I DIDN'T COME
TO SAY GOODBYE!

Navigating
the psychology
of immortality

By Moss A. Jackson, Ph.D.

ISBN 978-0-692-75839-7

EDITING: Joe Bardin and Karen Kinnison
PROOFREADING: Cynthia Joudrey
COVER DESIGN: Cool Line Design - Claudia Giménez
BOOK DESIGN: Cool Line Design - Claudia Giménez

Printed in United States of America
by Author2Market division of D&L Press
Phoenix, Arizona

Dedicated to my good friends and visionaries

JAMES STROLE
and BERNADEANE

ACKNOWLEDGMENTS

I want to thank Joe Bardin for his help in conceptualizing and editing this book, and Claudia Giménez for her wonderful design on the cover and throughout. Thanks also to my wife, Judy, for her sharp eyed review.

I'm grateful to Jim Strole and Bernadeane for their inspiration, and for introducing me to radical life extension and physical immortality.

Lastly, my love and appreciation to the People Unlimited community for their courage, warmth, integrity and commitment to embracing their unlimited potential.

TABLE OF CONTENTS

Forward   I-II

Introduction   1

How the Book is Laid Out   15

Chapter 1   How Does a Chick Know When
             to Peck its Way Out of an Egg?   21

Chapter 2   You Deserve to Live
             an Extraordinary Life   27

Chapter 3   Is Your Life an Investment or a Cost?   41

Chapter 4   The Survivor   49

Chapter 5   The Victim   55

Chapter 6   Are You a Navigator, Survivor or a Victim?   61

Chapter 7   Change, Radical Life Extension
             and Immortality   67

Chapter 8   Your Brain Holds The Key   89

Chapter 9   Life Sucks!   99

Chapter 10   Thoughts are Physical   111

Chapter 11   The Power of Belief   119

Chapter 12   Do You Like the Movies?   129

Chapter 13   The Body is a Map of the Mind   137

Chapter 14   Anchors of Anxiety   149

Chapter 15	A Cherokee Legend	157
Chapter 16	Breakthrough to Health, Vitality and Life	163
Chapter 17	Breakthrough Thinking	181
Chapter 18	The Rewiring of the Brain	193
Chapter 19	Your Emotional Brain and its Appetites	201
Chapter 20	Feeding Your Reptilian Brain	217
Chapter 21	What is the Value of Feeding the Triune Brain?	227
Chapter 22	The Art of Life Navigation	233
Chapter 23	Regrets, Grievances and Lost Opportunities	259
Chapter 24	You Deserve to Live an Extraordinary Life Now	267
Epilogue		275
Addendum		285
Poem: *Vision* by Lorna Collett		296
References		298
About the Author		300

FORWARD

Thank you, Moss, for writing this much needed book.

We're at a point in our development as humans where we have to look beyond the old mortality paradigm, and prepare ourselves psychologically, emotionally and physically to embrace our true potential for unlimited lifespans. And Moss Jackson has a unique skillset to help make this happen.

Moss is not only an extraordinary psychologist who has helped many people navigate their lives to a better, more productive place; he's a pioneer in the psychology of immortality. I believe this is the first book of its kind written — a practical, user-friendly guide for embracing radical life extension on a personal level.

Moss is also a great story teller, as you'll soon read in this book wherein he shares his very personal experiences, from childhood till now, about how it feels to have a strong life urge, be born into a world filled with death, and pilot your way to greater possibilities.

This book is a must read for anyone who is interested in finding their way to an extended life span, or simply to a more satisfying, emotionally healthy existence, which by the way, also has a direct effect on physical longevity. This book can help you navigate through the many obstacles and distractions that can detour you from the most important goal of all — STAYING ALIVE AND BEING HEALTHY.

Moss breaks it down into some simple but profound terms, which I hope will stir your consciousness to a new place, and help you become aware, if you aren't already, that we are at the dawn of a new era — the age of radical life extension and physical immortality.

There has never been a more exciting time to be alive, and we have the capacity to enjoy it to the fullest. Or we can keep replaying the same old survival patterns of anxiety, conflict and separation. This book clearly illustrates the choices we face, as well as providing practical strategies for selecting the routes that lead to greater authenticity, personal satisfaction and, of course, longevity.

James Strole
Director, People Unlimited
Director, Coalition for Radical Life Extension.

I DIDN'T COME TO SAY GOODBYE!

INTRODUCTION

I am not going to die!

I remember saying this as a child growing up in Brooklyn. Back then, the thought of dying seemed incomprehensible to me, ridiculous even. As a small child, I had an unshakable faith in everyone and everything that would protect me from death: my parents (especially my anxious mother), medicine, God, science and sometimes even chocolate. I knew that animals and people died, but how could I share the same fate? It wasn't possible. Yes, one might say that I was delusional as a young boy about my imagined freedom from death. Yet, I felt a deep and powerful truth inside of me, like a strong and invincible river current, invisible to the naked eye. While the surface currents were clearly visible, this deeper force was inviolate. Unshakable. Infinite.

I was fascinated and drawn to dead animals and insects. In my neighborhood stood tall and powerful oak trees, the permanent residences of a world of squirrels, birds and imperious insects. Sometime, I would come across a dead squirrel or bird, pick it up and carefully examine it. I was fascinated by the fact that something once living was now dead. Sometime, I would bring the unfortunate animal back to my apartment where I would wrap it in a warm towel, place some food near its mouth or blow air in its face, hoping to revive it back to life. It was an amazing mystery. *How could this once vibrant animal go from leaping stealthily from branch to branch to now so limp, powerless and dead?* I just did not get it! Death was incomprehensible and aberrant.

"There must be a secret formula," I thought, trying in vain to revive these unfortunate creatures.

I imagined that somehow, somewhere, someone knew the solution to death. I decided to find that person and use his discovery for myself in order to live forever.

I tried asking my mom if she knew the secret to living forever. One day, I brought a dead squirrel to her thinking that she would know what to do. After all, she was a nurse in a hospital for people with tuberculosis and cancer. She must know the secret to life. Yet, when I showed her the dead animal, she shuddered in horror and ordered, "Take it outside right now and throw it in the garbage!"

So, I reluctantly cast the poor soul into the garbage, thinking I would retrieve it later and experiment with life resuscitation. Of course, I failed miserably to bring it back to life. Frustrated, I thought my mother was lying to me, unwilling to share this secret because I was a child and children were not capable of using this magical skill wisely. She simply told me to go wash my hands while she prepared for me a tuna sandwich and some milk. We did not discuss it further that day.

My father provided a different perspective on human vulnerability. When I was about 10 years old, I would often ask him to play catch with me. Baseball was my passion; I loved the 1950s Brooklyn Dodgers. When they played a game, I would stand by our black-and-white TV, glove on, fielding imaginary grounders with ease and grace just like Pee Wee Reese at shortstop. I would scoop up the imaginary ball, pivot and throw the runner out at first base.

During these times, my dad would be sitting in his soft, comfortable chair with a scotch in one hand and his cherry tobacco-filled pipe in the other. After one particularly exciting game on TV, I turned to him, excitedly. "Dad, let's play catch," I said.

He inhaled on his well-chewed pipe and said, "I don't think that is a good idea. You know, the doctor told me not to exert myself because of the heart condition. You go out and play and I'll stay here reading my paper."

I was stunned by his refusal to play. It was, after all, only a game of catch. I mean, we "guys" and guys from Brooklyn, especially, played ball. I wasn't asking him to run around or do jumping jacks. I was both hurt and annoyed by his refusal. It didn't occur to me that he was really ill or would suffer any real damage if we threw the ball back and forth for a little bit. I left the apartment, ran downstairs from our fifth-story walk-up, threw open the main door and escaped into the alleyway. There, I hurled the ball against the brick wall and became absorbed in my fantasy play, quickly forgetting my dad and what he had said to me about his heart.

One year later, my father had his first heart attack. This was the first of many that he would suffer until his death at the untimely age of 59. That first attack made a powerful impression on me.

I was 11 years old and still a devoted Dodgers fan. That day, I was in my room when I heard my mom scream in the den. Racing into the room, I saw Dad sitting on the couch in his shorts and undershirt, sweating and looking very pale. He was holding his chest, panting and breathing quickly in short breaths. I asked my mom what was happening. She simply said "Your father is having a heart attack and I need to call an ambulance." Calm and focused, she acting as if nothing serious was going on, like she was handling some small task that required her attention. Mom was very efficient when it came to emergencies. She took care of things without much emotion or fanfare. At the same time, my dad's eyes flickered tearfully with fear and confusion.

Moments later, the ambulance arrived and the emergency team began to work on my dad. They took his blood pressure, then administered oxygen to him through a face mask. He continued to breathe with difficulty while looking at me with a distressed expression. Within minutes, they carried him out on a stretcher and into the ambulance. I watched with fascination as they worked their magic. His color improved, as did his breathing.

Soon, the ambulance whisked him away with my mother in attendance, while I remained in the apartment with my baseball glove firmly fixed on my hand. I fell asleep on the couch. Later, Mom returned home and put me to bed.

The next morning at breakfast, everything seemed to be back to normal, except for my father's absence. When I asked about him, my mom reassured me that he was fine and would be staying at the hospital for a week or two until he felt better. Taking her lead, I carried on with my day. I gathered up my books and school supplies and left for school.

When Dad returned home, little was said about the incident. He eventually went back to work as a salesman and resumed his daily schedule of drinking scotch, smoking his pipe and sitting in his chair. He did not change any of his habits. He refused to exercise or eat healthy foods.

To complicate the health issues even more, my mother was a terrible cook. A typical dinner consisted of lamb chops covered with "gravy," which consisted of fat drippings from the meat, along with mashed potatoes loaded with salt and butter, buttered biscuits, a glass of soda, and rich chocolate cake. It all tasted really good, but each meal was loaded with carbs, fat, sugar, and salt. I could picture every meal adding to my father's body as he steadily gained weight.

Even as a young child, I knew his sedentary lifestyle, combined with my mother's cooking, was like a time bomb ticking away toward disaster. Eventually, indeed, his life was cut short and he died when I was 29. During these years before his death, I would talk to him and my mother about the need for better eating, exercise and reducing the level of stress in the household. Yet, it all fell on deaf ears.

"It's Jewish cooking," my mom said. "Jews have cooked this way for thousands of years. What's the problem?"

Realizing they wouldn't change, I took on the responsibility of working out my own sensible eating habits and exercising. My goal was to eventually find the formula for health, well-being and life extension elsewhere, knowing it would not be within my family.

Much later, after college, my life shifted away from my family of origin to having my own family. I enrolled in graduate school and received my Ph.D. in Clinical Psychology. Upon graduation, I entered into private practice where I have enjoyed a prosperous and exciting career for many years. I loved my patients and focused on helping both myself and others live successful lives of productivity and good health.

As time passed, I continued to research and practice what I called "Life Navigation," the art of living with purpose, action and resilience. In 2010, I wrote my first book, *Navigating for Success: Passion, Goals and Action.* The basis for this book was the belief that everyone deserved to live an extraordinary life — one of success, accomplishment and satisfaction. Having learned some valuable lessons during my 30 years of practice, I wanted to share these insights with others. I still retained the belief from childhood that somehow I would not ever die. I was healthy, successful and adventurous. "What do I have to worry about?" I thought.

Then, in 2009, I noticed a disturbing sensation in my body. I felt an uncontrollable itch from my head to my toes, as if there were tiny insects crawling right below my skin. My doctor ordered an endoscopy, a procedure where a small camera is fed down the throat and into the digestive system. When I awoke from the procedure, the digestive physician and the radiologist informed my wife and me that some irregular cells were discovered in the bile tract and pancreas. The probable diagnosis was pancreatic cancer, one of the worst cancers to contract. Without chemotherapy and radiation, my life expectancy was less than six months. I could not believe the diagnosis. I thought the doctors were seriously mistaken. Yes, I had the skin irritation and there was an observable obstruction at the head of the pancreas, but there was no way I would die.

I quickly contacted several healers and the head of Therapheresis, a California research company that was conducting some new and non-invasive treatment approaches to curing cancer. At the same time, I met with Dr. Jeff Drebin, head of Gastrointestinal Surgery at the University of Pennsylvania Hospital and Dr. Foo at Sloan Kettering in New York. Both concurred that the diagnosis of pancreatic cancer was accurate and that surgery was immediately required. If not, I would probably die a terrible death sometime that year.

Although I still held onto my belief of never dying, I decided to have the surgery, a procedure called The Whipple. The Whipple was an extensive surgery where about a third of your pancreas is removed, along with your gallbladder and approximately 10 feet of the intestines. In all, it is a very serious procedure that necessitates a long recovery period and substantial changes in diet and lifestyle.

Two interesting things happened from this procedure that would have a powerful impact on me afterwards. One occurred when I was lying in bed awake three days after the surgery. It was about three in the morning and

I was feeling uncomfortable from the after effects of the surgery and medications. I was on my iPad looking for hypnotic inductions, imagery and relaxation exercises I could practice in my healing process. Hospitals tend to be noisy places, even at three in the morning. Sleep tends to be fitful and pain more intense.

As I skimmed through the online resources, I became aware that the room had become very quiet, as did the rustling and foot traffic from the doctors, nurses and aids out in the hallway. In fact, everything came to a standstill of absolute silence. I glanced up from my computer and looked around. To my surprise, I saw two small human-like figures standing in the hallway. They were about three feet tall, with very white skin and dressed in monk-like brownish, hooded cloaks. They quietly stared at me in a shy sort of way, appearing not to know how to approach me. I stared back at them with deep curiosity and interest. Amazingly, I felt no fear!

We stayed in joint visual embrace for several minutes, at which point I pulled myself up to a sitting position and said, "Thanks for coming but I am not ready to go!"

They quietly backed out of the room and vanished from sight. I took in a deep breath and resumed my iPad work. I thought little of it except to reaffirm my belief in my own immortality. Quite a curious experience, I thought.

A week later, I was discharged and sent home to recuperate for a month or two. Ten days later, I received an astonishing phone call from Dr. Drebin, my surgeon. He asked me to sit down because he needed to tell me something important. I totally expected bad news and perhaps even a death sentence.

After a brief pause, he said the following: "Moss, I have only had this conversation one time in a hundred. I have done 400 Whipples and you are the fourth person I am saying this to. You do not have cancer. Your tumor was not malignant. It was just a simple, benign growth. Unfortunately, we made a mistake. It fooled all of us and I'm really sorry for all of your discomfort."

His comments floored me, not because of the mistaken diagnosis but because of the terrific news. I did not have cancer! I was right to think I was immortal. I was just a healthy guy with a sore digestive system.

My diagnosis was autoimmune inflammatory disease of unknown origin. A little discomfort was well worth the result. No death for me!

I felt a renewed sense of vitality and optimism. I quickly launched back into my clinical work and rehab program. My belief in personal health re-energized my life and vitality. Although weakened, I felt hopeful and looked forward to navigating into a great life.

All of us, sooner or later, are confronted by bad news of our own mortality. It has been this way since life manifested on the planet. All living forms die, be they single-cell organisms, trees, hydras, coral reefs, mammals or whatever. No one or thing has ever escaped the inevitability of death. So far, there has been no immortality except in religion, where it exists as a hoped for after-death experience.

As I treat, coach and just talk with my clients, I remain curious about their personal perspectives and how they choose to journey throughout their individual lives. I have shared with many people my personal experiences with anxiety, illness and death, along with the decisions I have made to stay in the game of life, rather than to give in to the game of death. They, in return, have let their guards down and talked to me about their fears and, sometimes even what sounded like an addiction to a Death Psychology, an urge to give in to the forces of despair and hopelessness.

While they do not succumb to actual death, many live lives of continual struggle, stress, reactivity, rage and limiting beliefs, a kind of death in life. For them, life is a battle and, often, an irresistible urge toward giving up. I think it takes an unusual spirit and a life determination to rebound from life's upsets and to keep moving forward into the unknown. It has been my privilege to be their companion and guide when they choose to break loose and live to the fullest.

Why do some succumb while others persevere and thrive? Why do some people who are given a bad medical prognosis die while others with the same diagnosis do not go along with the physician's prediction, say "No thanks, not going there," recover and get on with their lives?

I, for one, am an advocate for life and never giving into the Death Psychology which we appear to be programmed to die into. I think there is a power of belief to provoke, create and to make life happen. We can become life provocateurs, Life Navigators, forces of nature who possess the power to continually break into new frontiers of living. We can envision possibilities, create opportunities to experiment and discover new tools and resources to propel us into extraordinary life experiences over and over again.

Every new expression of this life force helps to alter our DNA, our genetic blueprint and to create new brain dynamics that, repeated over time, organize our neural matrices and bodily cells into living extraordinary lives of success, accomplishment, satisfaction and considerable quality for many years.

My intention is to provide you with a powerful way of thinking and taking responsibility for your emotional and physical well-being, rewiring your brain and setting the stage for your own immortality.

What I learned from my three powerful experiences only confirmed what I knew so long ago as a young child. I had and still have an indomitable will to live. In the process, I have discovered some important lessons about health, stress and anxiety, resilience and life extension that I would like to share with you in this book.

The key purpose driving this book is the question, "How can we live extraordinary lives of success, accomplishment, satisfaction and life extension past the predictable time of our own death?"

I think there is much to be gained from the psychological perspective that can add both quality and actual years to your life. Perhaps medical technology will eventually provide us the resources for radical life extension, taking us to 125, 250, perhaps even 1,000 and into the realm of immortality.

Until then, we have some personal work to do. Hopefully you can share in the vision, *I Didn't Come to Say Goodbye.* May these techniques and ideas help you live a long and resilient life, one where death is resisted, personal adventures are pursued and longevity is prolonged.

I mean, if the Brooklyn Dodgers — known for years as "Dem Bums"— could resurrect and beat the indomitable New York Yankees in the 1954 World Series, our physical immortality is possible.

HOW THE BOOK IS LAID OUT

I Didn't Come to Say Goodbye! is written to give you a useful template for living an extraordinary long and healthy life of success, accomplishment and satisfaction.

The FIRST CHAPTER, **"How Does a Chick Know When to Peck its Way Out of an Egg?"** is about choices, change and risk-taking. Too often, people marinate in a reactive lifestyle that leads to stress, disease and a shortened lifespan. Others, Life Navigators, chart a life course and take timely actions that lead to a sense of control, safety and satisfaction.

CHAPTER TWO, **"You Deserve to Live an Extraordinary Life,"** focuses on the key questions "What do you love about your life?" and "What are you grateful for?"

CHAPTER THREE, **"Is Your Life an Investment or a Cost?,"** covers the life of a Navigator, a powerful lifestyle that results in extraordinary living, success, accomplishment and satisfaction.

CHAPTERS FOUR AND FIVE, **"The Survivor"** and **"The Victim,"** provide two other lifestyles more closely related to stressful living, immunological breakdown and illness.

CHAPTER SIX, **"Are You a Navigator, Survivor or a Victim?"** provides an opportunity to take a self-scoring questionnaire that will help you better understand your journey through life.

In CHAPTER SEVEN, **"Change, Radical Life Extension and Immortality,"** we learn that change can bring both crisis and opportunity. The transition into radical life extension and immortality is enormous, a change that will push humans into Breakthrough Thinking and major life adjustments.

In CHAPTER EIGHT, **"Your Brain Holds the Key,"** the Triune brain is described, along with how it developed over 400 million years. This development takes us through the Reptilian, Primate, and Homo Sapien brains, all of which must find a way of coexisting inside our nervous system.

CHAPTER NINE, **"Life Sucks!"**, is oriented to show that we are more wired to experience anxiety and worry rather than ease and optimism, and the greater case against living life as a Navigator.

In CHAPTER TEN, **"Thoughts Are Physical,"** we examine the powers of our thoughts and beliefs in determining our health or illness. Thoughts are real, can be measured and tracked, and can even result in bodily chaos and the breakdown of coherence and resilience. It all depends on what and how you are thinking.

CHAPTER ELEVEN, **"The Power of Belief,"** takes us further into how powerful beliefs directly impact our destiny and life quality.

In CHAPTER TWELVE, **"Do You Like the Movies?",** we look at deception and illusion in our lives and how our lives are like a movie. Reality may be something very different from how most people understand it.

In CHAPTER THIRTEEN, **"The Body is a Map of the Mind,"** CHAPTER FOURTEEN, **"Anchors of Anxiety,"** and CHAPTER FIFTEEN, **"A Cherokee Legend,"** we examine how our thoughts, beliefs, and values further deepen our life experience.

CHAPTERS SIXTEEN through EIGHTEEN take us into **"Breakthrough to Health, Vitality and Life," "Breakthrough Thinking,"** and **"The Rewiring of the Brain."** The four key questions that Life Navigators carefully examine and answer are discussed. In order to live into the possibility of radical life extension — to add 25 healthy years to your life — one must adopt a radically different way of thinking.

In CHAPTER NINETEEN, **"Your Emotional Brain and its Appetites,"** CHAPTER TWENTY, **"Feeding Your Reptilian Brain"**, and CHAPTER TWENTY-ONE, **"What is the Value of Feeding the Triune Brain?"**, the key nutrients of Power, Connection and Safety are examined as they relate to brain vitality.

CHAPTER TWENTY-TWO, **"The Art of Life Navigation,"** describes the advantages the Life Navigator has over the Survivor and the Victim: his success formula and the powerful foods of Power, Connection and Safety.

CHAPTER TWENTY-THREE, **"Regrets, Grievances and Lost Opportunities,"** explores the five key regrets of people close to death.

CHAPTER TWENTY-FOUR, **"You Deserve to Live an Extraordinary Life Now,"** summarizes a Navigator's perspective on living an extraordinary life and how you can take more control of your life quality and longevity.

There are two additional chapters: an epilogue and an addendum.

In the **"Epilogue,"** we examine how humans stay stuck even when they do not have to.

In the **"Addendum,"** there are several experimental exercises you can take to experience an emotional and bodily sense of radical life extension, integrating the Computer, Gorilla and Alligator minds so that they work together for your continued health and resilience. The third exercise presents how your Computer, your thinking brain, might try to navigate a conflict between the Gorilla and Alligator brains.

Chapter 1:

HOW DOES A CHICK KNOW WHEN TO PECK ITS WAY OUT OF AN EGG?

All chicks grow and develop inside eggs. It seems a rather simple matter. The embryo grows into a small chick while it takes in the highly nutritious fluids inside its egg. The tiny chick thrives in this rich environment, each day growing stronger and developing further. Time continues to pass until the chick is ready for its departure from its safe home into the world outside the egg. But not all chicks leave the egg. While many finally make it out, there are quite a few who stay inside too long and perish.

Why is it that some succeed and others do not? Does each chick have a choice to stay or leave? If a chick chose to remain in its nurturing world, what eventually becomes of it? Does it grow and then just retire in its protective world of the egg? Or does it shrivel up and perish for some strange reason?

One interesting theory is that while its original environment is nourishing and delicious, it gradually becomes less and less nourishing as each day passes. Each day the chick excretes waste back into its home base. Therefore, its dinner becomes rather foul tasting and harmful to the growing chick. Gradually, there comes a tipping point where the rich feeding world of the egg becomes so toxic that the growing chick turns its attention to the surrounding shell and pecks its way out into the outside world.

If the chick remains too long it perishes because the waste becomes greater than its food. Consequently, the chick weakens more and more each passing day until it eventually dies. As one chick thrives as it pecks its way into the external world to begin life's adventures, the other chick dies in its own excrement.

THE WAITING GAME

Some of us are those chicks who wait too long in life environments, lifestyles, destructive relationships and behavioral patterns that eventually wear us down and cause serious emotional and physical breakdown. While these patterns might have had value at some earlier time in our lives, they can become stagnant and self-destructive if held onto without fresh critical analyses and change.

So, for all you humans, don't wait too long in your pain, anxiety and misery. Take action as early as you can and leap into your future. Take a risk like the chick and get on with your life. After all, you deserve to live an extraordinary life, one of success, accomplishment, happiness and longevity.

In life, we have choices. On the one hand, there is a life of reactivity, a life of waiting: waiting until something gets better, until you catch a "break" and your fortune happens, until you get noticed, promoted or finally appreciated. Waiting until you graduate or get married, have children or get rid of your children. Maybe even waiting until you die.

» How bad do things have to get before you decide to make a change and take effective action?

» How sick do you have to become before you decide to change your lifestyle, start eating well, or improve your sleep or exercise regime on a regular basis?

» How much more stress will you take on before you finally say "enough" and shift your life into a less tense and chronically stressed life?

» How miserable do things have to get before you force your way out of the shell in which you are now trapped?

You do not have to wait until illness, exhaustion and anxiety overwhelm your natural resources and defense structures. Like a chick who waits too long and delays its exit strategy into a new life, some individuals wait too long to change and continue to marinate in a stressful and unhealthy lifestyle. These people get weaker and weaker by the day, until they finally succumb to chronic stress and fall into ill health, depression or broken spirits.

THE EARLY ADOPTERS

Others, let's call them the early adopters of healthy living, shift into a mindful and conscientious lifestyle before everything falls apart. They focus on finding more responsible ways to take care of themselves. They are the life experimenters, taking on new challenges and stepping outside their comfort zones. They are practitioners of mindfulness, heart breathing, alternative medicine and other life enhancing practices. They are learning to step outside their critical and negative mindsets, working to "peck" out of their old emotionally exhausting patterns of unhealthy living. They are discovering new breakthroughs in their own neuroplasticity and rewiring their brains, even to the point of altering the aging process.

They are Navigators of Immortality, curious and inventive about life and open to finding new ways to break out of the "Death Psychology" of waiting, reactivity or just tolerating what life throws at them.

In the not-too-distant future, and sooner than we think, science and technology will bring us new breakthroughs into longevity, radical life extension and, eventually, age reversal. Until then, we have a lot of work to do to prepare for our future.

Each of us has a choice to stay inside our shells and comfort zones or choose to take action and "push" our way into the new science of life extension and anti-aging. If we wait too long, sickness and physical breakdown will win out. If we shift now, we can set the stage for our future well-being by preparing ourselves to meet science half way while we are still healthy enough to reap the benefits that await us. We can live into vitality and aliveness instead of waiting for life to get better.

Key Points

- Don't spend too long a time in toxic environments or relationships

- Action is the best antidote to anxiety and misery

- You deserve to live an extraordinary life

- You do not have to wait until illness and anxiety become overwhelming to take action

- Early adapters of healthy living take responsibility for their lives

- Early adapters do not rely on hope, good intentions or good deeds to save the day

- Create your own vitality and aliveness instead of waiting for life to get better

Chapter 2:

YOU DESERVE TO LIVE AN EXTRAORDINARY LIFE

» What do you love about your life?

» Who and what are you grateful for?

» What do you appreciate most about your life?

» How do you express your love and appreciation?

When you meet someone, how do you usually greet and what do you both talk about? If you are like most others, it comes down to something like this: "Hi, my name is Moss; I live near Philadelphia and work as a psychologist and success coach. How about you? What are you up to nowadays?"

Most social conversations run along these lines — pretty nondescript and quite forgettable. It is part-and-parcel of our social convention. The bulk of our conversations are very predictable and basically boring! There is little to capture one's interest or curiosity. But it serves a basic function which is to create the impression or illusion of making a connection without making any commitment or taking much of a personal risk.

THE PASSION CONVERSATION

On the other hand, what if you stepped out of social convention and started a conversation by saying something like the following: "Hi, my name is Moss. What do you love about your life? What's creating passion and excitement for you?" Or perhaps something like, "If you could push a magic button and live this next year with love and passion, what would your life look like?"

When I travel by plane to a conference or a speaking engagement, I might say to the person sitting next to me: "You know, I'm on my way to talk about living an extraordinary life of success, accomplishment and satisfaction. I was wondering what you love about your life? Would you be willing to share your thoughts with me?"

When I first considered entering into this kind of personal conversation, I had some misgivings:

"Would the person be offended by my questions?"

"Since I do not know this person, maybe I should just play it safe."

"Perhaps I could offer a piece of gum and ask what the person is reading."

"Maybe I should just stay absorbed in what I'm reading and avoid conversation. I don't want to create discomfort for my neighbor or myself."

"Then again, there must be something I could say that might add some value in the conversation."

A few years ago, for example, I was flying back from Columbus, Ohio, where I had attended a conference with a number of my colleagues.

I was settled down with a book about halfway back to Philadelphia when I glanced at the book my neighbor was reading. It was a book on personal growth by Wayne Dyer. I mentioned I had recently completed reading the same book and commented on some personal value I had gained from the book. He shared what he liked about the book in return.

The conversation deepened as we discussed his insights and learning. He shared with me some issues he was working on both personally and professionally. About twenty minutes from landing, I asked him the question, "If you could push a magic button and live this next year with love and passion, what would your life look like?"

During the rest of the flight, my companion expressed his concerns, desires and visions to live a more fulfilled personal life and to be a better leader in his company.

Time flew by as his thoughts, aspirations and dreams came tumbling out. It seemed like only moments had passed before we landed.

As we walked together toward the baggage claim area, our conversation continued and deepened. He expressed his concerns about growing older and his wish to leave a legacy of rebuilding his business culture. I listened attentively while offering no advice or solution. I was just a container for his passions and wishes.

As we parted, I gave him a copy of my new book *Navigating for Success: Passion, Goals and Actions* and suggested he might find something of value in reading it. He seemed to appreciate the gift and said he would gladly do so, and then asked if it would be okay for him to reach out to me after he read the book. I smiled and said I would enjoy the follow-up.

That incident took place almost six years ago and we have stayed in touch since that time on a regular basis. I have worked with him and his teams to help create the cultural impact he had described in our conversation on the plane. It is astonishing how that one crucial question about passion and desire transformed a transient plane conversation into such a rich and personally satisfying ongoing relationship.

To my surprise and delight, I discovered that rather than upsetting or offending anyone, the vast majority of people become instantly engaged by these questions. Through these conversations with strangers, I came to appreciate how hungry others were to talk about their dreams and joys, often thanking me or asking for my business card before we said our goodbyes. More than a few times, I followed up these highly interesting conversations with opportunities to coach or counsel people during the next year. Sometimes, I would send my new friends an article or book recommendation that complemented what they had talked about during those first connections. Often, they would reach out to me to communicate their appreciation about either our conversation or what I had sent them in my follow-up contact.

PLAYING IT SAFE

If most of us want to live a great life, one of love, passion and satisfaction, why is it that we are so hesitant to let others know about our passions?

Why do we play it safe and hide out in our private thoughts, only to share them with a few discreet people we trust and feel safe with?

Perhaps it comes from a fear of being intrusive or too personal, or a concern of being looked at as a jerk or someone on the Autism Spectrum, a condition in which a person may come across as socially awkward or immature. Many are stuck in a cocoon of playing it safe and fearful of humiliation, thinking, "Better safe than sorry, so just keep your real insights and feelings to yourself."

Have you noticed how most young children do not play it safe? They jump around, interrupt our serious conversations to show us something they made or are doing. They make noise and flail about, demanding our total attention. They express passion and excitement without any apparent concern for propriety, good manners or looking good. Do you remember when you were such a kid?

What happened over time?

» How did the vast majority of us become so serious, uptight, reserved and careful?

» Is there still a trace of passion, silliness and freshness inside you that yearns to come out and play?

» Let's imagine that someone had the courage to ask you what you love and value about your life. What would you answer?

For me, I love my wife, Judy, and my children. They bring me great joy and satisfaction. Just thinking about them sends my dopamine production into high drive. When I picture each of them and allow that picture to linger in my visual imagery and feel myself re-experiencing it, I feel even more satisfaction. They give me such a strong sense of joy and gratitude that even thinking about them reconnects me to them at an emotional level.

I also love my work and my patients. I have deep appreciation for the trust and confidence they instill in me and the transparency and self-expression that they share with me each week.

I also value my curiosity and love of learning. I love writing and researching topics such as the one I am now writing about. I love my resiliency and sense of aliveness.

I so appreciate when I "forget myself," my age, status and all the other restraining forces that keep me in my shell, and just "let go" with my felt experience of passion, pleasure and excitement. I can then feel my playful child rejoicing inside me, standing and cheering me on to express myself to others who ask how I am doing.

WHAT ABOUT YOU?

How about you? How would you answer this question:

» What do you love and value about your life?

I suggest you take a few minutes to think about your answers and even write them down. Also, take a moment to pause and linger on the answer as you imagine your experience with a loved one or something you enjoy doing.

For the next couple of weeks, take a few moments each day to reflect on the question. Just thinking about it will probably have a very positive effect on your nervous system. Your reflections on the things you love about life will activate the pleasure centers in your brain, reduce your stress and anxiety and increase your sense of well-being. Try sharing your answers with your loved ones and close companions. Then, ask them what they love about their lives.

Often, we become so activated by the circumstances of our everyday lives and find ourselves jumping from one upset or problem to another. Some of my patients describe their lives like they are the metal balls in a pinball machine, bouncing back and forth between the tight rubber bands and the ringing bells. Going through the day and dealing with problematic situations can exhaust you and lead you to question whether you were able to accomplish much of anything during the day. What a loss of vitality to be living a life of reactivity and chronic stress.

This is the "Death Psychology" that is the price of getting stuck and not living into a thriving and nurturing life energy.

SOMETIMES OUR MINDS BEAT US UP

Research suggests we have around 60,000 unconscious thoughts a day, 80 percent of which are negative. On a conscious level, we have about 2,500 thoughts, 2,000 of which are negative. Thoughts could be about what your schedule looks like, things you want or do not want to do, about what you do or do not want to see, or, you may be concerned about a bill or conversation you have to handle, your weight and health, a phone call you need to return, a meeting you have to attend.

You might find yourself repeating the same thoughts, concerns and hopes many times during the day without taking action. These internal expressions can be fleeting, lasting a few seconds or, then again, they can stick to you like Velcro and resist leaving you alone. In any case, without conscious effort, most people are bombarded by waves of thought that frequently add little real value to their lives and interactions.

And 90 percent of these thoughts we probably repeat the next day!

This tendency, along with approximately 50 stress points each day, does not lead to much pleasure or satisfaction. To experience a sense of success and pleasure, we have to take a *time out*, a pause to reflect on what makes us feel good about our lives.

Asking yourself what you love about your life each day is an excellent way to remind yourself that you are okay and your life is working. This then becomes the context or lens through which you experience your day. Sometimes we need a nudge to keep us on the path of vitality and well-being. You have to feel good to even want to live a radically extended life, much less to make it happen.

VICTORY LOG

Another strategy is to keep a victory log each day. Toward the end of the day, take a few minutes and write in a notebook or journal what victories you experienced each day. These victories do not have to be big or important. They can simply be the small things that you experienced or shared with others.

For me, an example of a victory could be that I asked my secretary how her day is going or how her husband is doing. Or it could be returning a phone call in a timely fashion or even paying a bill. Another could be calling a patient after a difficult session to ask how they're doing.

People feel appreciated and valued by such expressions and I consider all of these small victories that go into my victory log.

GRATITUDES

You might also practice Gratitudes every day. What are you grateful for? When we are in an upset mood, or feeling down, it may seem difficult to identify the positives in your life. However, with a little practice, you will be able to list a multitude of things both small and large for which you are grateful.

I invite you to recite five Gratitudes each morning as part of your morning ritual, perhaps even before you get out of bed. With each gratitude, let yourself appreciate and savor your thoughts and feelings. As you feel the experience, appreciate the fact that you are allowing some dopamine, your feel-good chemical, to be secreted and nourish every cell in your body — all one hundred trillion of them!

Be a Moses feeding the throngs of hungry Hebrew slaves escaping from the pharaoh's cruelty in Egypt. He fed the throngs of people with hope and the future promise of milk and honey. Feed your 100 trillion cells with a few Gratitudes. They can help you to better travel the miles you will experience during the day. What better preparation is there for living forever?

These simple conversations and practices can go a long way to redesigning your nervous system to become more relaxed, energized and resilient. What a gift for yourself! Repeated on a daily basis, you are laying down new neural pathways and creating the groundwork for a healthier, and perhaps, more extended life.

Key Points

- Stop being boring in your relationships and conversations.

- Ask others what they love about their lives.

- Become more generous.

- Stop playing it safe and worrying about what others think about you. Most people are paying attention to themselves, not you!

- Keep a daily victory log.

- If you find yourself bombarded by negative thoughts, pause and write them down. The worst place to keep them is in your head. Writing them down creates distance from your thoughts and can sometimes help you see how exaggerated and outlandish your fears and worries can be.

- Recite and savor five things for which you are grateful.

- Give your body a dopamine "feel-good" experience as often as possible. Here's how: Find something during the day to appreciate. Savor the experience for 30 seconds and let it settle in. Reviewing the experience rewires your brain to feel good and have an extraordinary day.

- Start acting silly!

Chapter 3:

IS YOUR LIFE AN INVESTMENT OR A COST?

Some people thrive in their lives, experiencing a sense of aliveness, adventure and success. Others fall into a perpetual state of survival. They can be seen struggling, overreacting and becoming overwhelmed by minor upsets. Though both types of individuals go through life, the quality of each life path is considerably different. Who would want to extend a life path of suffering?

THE NAVIGATOR

Those who thrive in their lives are called Navigators (Jackson, 2010). The Navigator has a clear sense of where he or she is going, what he wants, and his purpose. The Navigator strives to enhance the quality of his life every day.

Resilient, he is able to cope with upsets as they arise by maintaining a sense of poise and composure. When he becomes frustrated, it is a temporary feeling. He manages the tension rising in his body, realizing that too much upset will throw him into illogical thinking, panic reactivity and poor decision making. He catches his breath, grounds himself and shifts into a problem-solving mode of thinking.

The Navigator appreciates that he lives in two worlds that need to be continually taken care of and integrated. The internal world is the one of personal self-regulation, of staying grounded, being reasonably calm, practicing slow and deep breathing and other physical self-caring actions.

The other world is the external environment where coping, problem-solving and relationship building are constantly requiring our attention.

The Navigator works to balance these two worlds, neither becoming so self-involved that he gets swallowed up in narcissistic self-absorption nor yanked out of control by external demands. He both copes and self-regulates.

You might be thinking that the Navigator's life is a walk in the park. This is not the case. Navigators face just as many obstacles and problems as everyone else. The key difference is that Navigators face these challenges with self-awareness, vision, focus, powerful coping strategies and even a sense of humor.

For example, rather than obsess over their mistakes, Navigators take responsibility for their screw ups, learn from their mistakes, review their options and take action. Even though they will continue to make mistakes in the future, Navigators will not likely make the same ones. With each mistake and learning, they continually rewire their neocortex and lay down more refined and elegant neural pathways to success.

Navigators are clear about where they are going and why they are going there. They resist slipping into the perilous territory of self-doubt and other forms of self-sabotage.

However, if they ever fall off track, they find a way to recover as soon as possible. They become masters of the mind battle. The mind battle is the relentless attack against our self-confidence from self-generated negative chatter. This chatter lingers inside all of us to diminish our confidence and courage. It is that critical chatter that tries to make us take things too personally, cling to self-defeating assumptions, catastrophize minor upsets and erect barriers to our success. Navigators confront their inner critics, dispute them and sometimes even laugh at them.

BRENDA: Realizing you deserve better

I have a patient, Brenda, who is working hard to become a Navigator. When I first met her two years ago, she was agitated, took things personally, was easily thrown into bouts of tears and anger. She lacked purpose and a sense of hope for her future.

In her personal life, she bounced from one partner to another without any clear idea of what she was seeking in them. She was overly accommodating and giving, thinking that other people would reciprocate in kind. Unfortunately, instead of finding a trusting relationship, she only found a string of men who seemed to take advantage of her kindness.

She was living life as a Survivor, a life of struggle, unsuccessful coping strategies and beliefs that her good will and deeds would eventually be rewarded in a loving relationship.

In our most recent meeting, she talked with clarity about a relationship that she had just terminated. She realized that she was giving more to the relationship than he was. There were other issues. She was adventurous while he was more traditional. There also were significant differences in sexual desire. After several months of trying to create a greater connection and to foster mutual care taking, Brenda realized that her boyfriend was mired in his old negative thinking patterns.

He would take things too personally, lash out when criticized and was uninterested in changing or growing. Stuck in a rigid pattern, he took no responsibility for his actions, so Brenda decided to end the relationship. Though she was somewhat disappointed, she was glad that she listened to the voice in her head that told her that she deserved better.

Brenda also discussed a work-related incident where she felt mistreated. For the first time in her life, she chose to confront the person with whom she was in conflict. She told her coworker that she was bothered by something and would like to discuss it so that they could improve their working relationship. When the coworker became defensive, Brenda acknowledged her feelings but quickly got back to the issue at hand.

Several times, she told her coworker that her intent was to find more mutually satisfying ways to work together rather than in competition. She also expressed that if they could not resolve their issue soon, she would be glad to have their supervisor join the discussion.

Luckily, they were able to resolve their issue, causing Brenda to feel confident and satisfied with her ability to adapt to stressors rather than just accommodate them and become emotionally overwhelmed.

Brenda was becoming a Navigator! She had direction, goals to achieve, strategies to take action and a strong capacity to self-regulate her emotional reactions and remain calm. She stated that she deserved to live an extraordinary life of success and satisfaction and was taking actions to realize these intentions. She was no longer living in a dream world hoping for rescue or miracles. She was using a formula for aliveness and success based on self-awareness, courage and personal responsibility.

REBOUNDING WITH PURPOSE

When Navigators experience distress and begin to slide into the world of reactivity and low confidence, they do not stay there very long. They challenge this way of operating and take actions aligned with their vision and purpose. They work to become the person who can face their challenges and even redesign their brains to make success attainable.

It is this assemblage of thought, planning, self-regulation and self-redesign that makes the Navigator's life so engaging, energizing and rewarding. By paying attention to the condition of their lives and adjusting their actions to complement their goals and life purpose, Navigators experience considerable levels of satisfaction.

Others notice the unique path of the Navigators because they appear more relaxed and in control of their destinies than the typical person. I imagine that their redesigned lifestyles and advanced skills go a long way to enhance both the quality and longevity of their lives.

In a later chapter we will look at how the Navigator's thinking patterns actually affect the hormones, neurotransmitters and chemistry in their bodies. Let's now look at two other lifestyles that are a cost rather than an investment.

Key Points

- Navigators have vision and know what they want.

- Navigators face the same number of stressors and negative thoughts as others.

- Navigators resist slipping into self-doubt and self-sabotage. They simply say "No" and shift their thinking onto a path that leads them to results, not suffering.

- Navigators are constantly learning and rewiring their brain. They learn by experience and redesign themselves to be the people they want to be.

- Rather than staying stuck in negative thinking, Navigators create action-oriented thoughts that open up life opportunities for success, connection and satisfaction.

- Navigators take the time to appreciate what gives them satisfaction.

- Navigators practice Gratitudes every day.

- Navigators take personal responsibility for their lives.

Chapter 4:

THE SURVIVOR

I have another patient, let's call him Eric, who is relatively successful but you wouldn't know it because he is constantly stressed and upset. For him, he views life as a daily battle where there are only winners and losers. That would be a hell of a way to live an unlimited life span.

After a difficult period of time many years back, he made a decision to never be a loser again. He was set on winning the battle of life no matter the cost. His subconscious motto was, "Get the other guy before he gets you!"

With this mindset, Eric was always alert to signs of attack, betrayal and others taking advantage of him. As most of us know, when you look for something, you will end up finding it.

He eventually began sensing threats from everyone, whether it was coworkers, family or friends. He went through life like a pit bull, ready to snap and lash out at anyone he perceived as a potential threat. His motto was, "Why take a chance? Strike before being stricken."

Consequently, there was a lot of "road kill" in Eric's life.

THE DISCONTENT OF SURVIVAL

Survivors are fighters. They endure adversity and prevail against all odds. As they elbow their way through life, they may amass considerable business and financial success, but, beyond the initial highs of winning, they do not usually feel lasting contentment.

All of us possess a Survivor identity to some extent. None of us are immune to pain and the hurts we have accumulated during our lifetimes. Occasionally, we encounter people who don't have our best interests in mind. In these situations, survivor traits are useful because they alert us to individuals and situations that might harm us.

It is in our personal self-interest to recognize any toxic relationship, whether personal, business or even familial, and deal with it appropriately. Do not put up with anyone's domination, disdain, passive aggressiveness, guilt-making or any behavior that diminishes your self-worth or personal well-being.

It is one thing to have a healthy dose of Survivor spirit within us, but quite another to live life as a Survivor 24 hours a day. Those who have assumed a survival way of life as their core identity have a hard time switching it off. Their internal alarm button that scans for threats will not allow it!

The alarm is always on, beeping and lighting up at any sign of potential harm, real or imagined. Ever sensitive to perceived hurts, Survivors see enemies where they do not exist. Consequently, they tend to send out negative energy such that others may react defensively to them, thus fulfilling the Survivor's expectation of probable harm or threat. They then feel righteous in their negative world view when others react negatively to them. As a result, they amp up their Survivor-based perceptions and actions, perpetuating a mutually dissatisfying experiential cycle.

THE COST OF LIVING LIFE AS A SURVIVOR

Let's now focus on the physical and biological consequences of living life as a Survivor. Remaining on constant alert for social threats produces profound effects in the body. Due to their inability to regulate their emotional fear states, Survivors secrete excess adrenaline and cortisol into their blood streams. Research suggests that short bursts of adrenaline or cortisol are useful, but the more these chemicals linger in our bodies, the more damaging they become. When an individual's stress levels remain high, these create a chronic attack on the body, placing the individual at risk for inflammation, reduced immunity, heart damage, and even shortened life spans.

When animals or humans sense danger, their fight-or-flight response gets tripped. Upon perceiving a threat, the brain sends a signal to the adrenal gland to create the hormones cortisol and adrenaline. These chemicals activate the heart rate and breathing rate to dilate blood vessels so that blood can quickly flow to the muscles in your legs and arms. Besides helping you to flee or fight, acute stress can boost the immune response for three to five days.

CHRONIC INFLAMMATION

Sometimes, Survivors have difficulty getting their physiological activation resettled after the fight-or-flight event is over. They may worry and remain agitated for a long time, setting themselves up for long-term problems. According to researcher Robert Sapolsky (2004), a Stanford University stress expert and author of *Why Zebras Don't Get Ulcers*, chronic and repeated stress may interfere with the immune system and even slow the healing of wounds. Chronic inflammation — that is, the immune system's response to injury or irritation — may be closely related to higher rates of heart disease and diabetes. So, indirectly, a stress-related imbalance in the immune system may have far-reaching effects on our health.

When the perceived threat is gone, the healthy response is for the Central Nervous System (CNS) to go back to a lower arousal level. If the CNS is continually bombarded by repeated cortisol spikes from stress, arousal remains high, the heart works harder, thus raising the risk of hypertension, stroke and heart attack. Moreover, Survivors under chronic stress are more susceptible to colds and viral illnesses.

The bottom line is that if you are a Survivor and have difficulty calming your nervous system down due to an inability to handle chronic stress, you are in danger of weakening your immune system, becoming sick, and ultimately risking not just your happiness, but your life.

Key Points

- Survivors are fighters.

- Survivors are not usually satisfied, content or happy.

- All of us need to have Survivor skills and use them when needed.

- Chronic Survivors suffer from excess adrenaline and cortisol spikes.

- Survivors may suffer from inflammation due to excessive demands on their immunological system.

- Living in a state of chronic stress arousal and Survival Mode Living can be habitual and resistant to re-calming and restoring your nervous system back to a stable state.

- Chronic survival actions cause negative reactions in others.

- Living a life of survival and chronic stress can kill you.

Chapter 5:

THE VICTIM

A third way that people go through life is in Victim mode. Unlike Survivors, Victims have already concluded that they can't win. They live in a perceived world of unfairness, helplessness and low self-efficacy or control. Victims tend to face challenges and obstacles with a sense of passivity and a "Why bother?" attitude. They frequently sigh and throw up their hands in surrender. Victims can be found saying or thinking, "No one really cares about me," "There is nothing I can do about it," and "This always happens to me."

THE WORLD OF THE VICTIM

In the world of the Victim, there is not much room for creativity or discovery. Their minds are made up, so why try something new? Taking risks and stepping out of their comfort zones has not worked in the past and they fear they will fail again. Many Victims crave the safety of predictability, habit and ritual. Consequently, Victims may be afraid to take on a promotion, seek a new job or move to another city. They may also fail to speak up for themselves, express their own opinions or disagree directly with others.

In many cases, Victims are not aware of their fears, paralyses or attachment to the status quo. They can easily drift into abusive relationships or jobs, remain chronically unhappy and fret that others do not seem interested in how they are doing. The fact is that others usually do not know how the Victim is doing because of the covert way the Victim lives. If he does not express his unhappiness or make requests, he stays stuck in his lonely and miserable circumstance.

A Victim's Story

Jim, a patient I saw a few years ago, told me a story that touched my heart. He had grown up with a cold, emotionally distant mother. We know from clinical experience that children who are raised by mothers who are distant and disconnected grow up with insecure attachments and are in danger of becoming emotionally distant or ambivalent themselves.

When Jim would rush home from school, eager to show his mother a picture he had drawn, she would stiffen up, glance dismissively at his work and say something like, "Stop with all this drawing nonsense and focus on your school work like you need to." Needless to say, Jim felt hurt and angry. He would then retreat to his room, alone with his overwhelming feelings. Jim, like most young children, never told his mother how he felt. Gradually, after repeated experiences such as this, he concluded he was not good enough or very lovable.

Although he performed well in school, he never felt like he was good enough. Rather than learn to give himself credit, Jim looked to others for approval and to gain a sense of his self. Consequently, others took advantage of him and his need to be liked. He never turned people down, helping acquaintances with their papers and reports. Though he assumed that helping others would grant him a sense of well-being, the opposite occurred. The more he accommodated people's requests and demands, the less worthy he felt.

As an adult, he took up with business associates who, like those before them, took advantage of Jim's good nature. Though Jim was concerned about the business deals, he was unable to confront his associates. Much to his chagrin, he eventually found himself near financial ruin. He was almost $3 million in debt, with several lawsuits piled up against him. His response was a predictable Victim-thought pattern: "Why do bad things always happen to me? It must have been my fault somehow."

What intrigued me about Jim were the contradictory landscapes in which he was living his life. He was truly brilliant. On the other hand, his choice of business partners was terrible. He had a pattern of partnering up with cold, narcissistic, manipulative men who would tell him how terrific he was while lining their pockets with the money he was bringing in. In a way, he was replaying his rejecting childhood relationship with his mother.

THE STRUGGLE OF SISYPHUS

Jim's situation reminded me of the Greek legend of Sisyphus, the man who angered the gods and was sentenced to push a giant boulder up a steep hill. If he could successfully push the boulder to the top of the hill only once and bring it to a rest, he would be freed from this onerous task. But Sisyphus could never quite make it to the top. He spent an eternity pushing the boulder up the hill, only to have it constantly roll back down before he could reach the summit.

Jim kept hoping that his diligent work and giving nature would bring him acknowledgment, respect and love. But, like Sisyphus, he never quite got his boulder to the hill's precipice.

When Jim came to see me, he was in very bad shape. He was near financial ruin, his marriage was in tatters, he was depressed and in deep legal difficulties. He had fallen so deeply into despair that it did not take much effort on my part to get him to grasp the futility of his Victim style. The thought of standing up for himself terrified him. He was sure that others would hurt him or reject him. He wished that if he could just try a little harder to accommodate their demands, then people wouldn't be mad with him and everything would be okay.

Gradually, through many slips and regressions, Jim learned to stop giving in to others, to speak for himself and stand his ground. He realized how addicted he was to the Victim identity and how deadly it was to his well-being, health and life.

After Jim put in the hard work to better himself, one of the first results was that his wife grew to respect him. He also learned how to better tolerate her disapproval without falling apart. Through this process, he came to have a better understanding of how his mother operated as a Survivor out of necessity, due to her own conditioning and belief structure which affected her ability to be the warm caregiver that he needed.

Also, Jim broke ties with the partners who were manipulating him and found more trustworthy people to work with. Jim learned that there were other ways to get through life than being the Victim.

Although the Victim style is considerably different than the Survivor, both styles are characterized by considerable stress, anxiety and unhappiness. In either case, damage is done to the spirit, body and mind. Both stressful lifestyles increase a person's risk for infections, inflammation, autoimmune dysfunction and sickness.

Key Points

- Victims feel powerless.

- Victims crave safety.

- Victims usually do not take responsibility for their misery. They blame others.

- Victims find themselves repeating rigid and self-defeating patterns.

- Victims can change.

- Victims do damage to their spirits, bodies and minds.

- Being a victim is not a healthy lifestyle.

Chapter 6:

ARE YOU A NAVIGATOR, SURVIVOR OR A VICTIM?

Now that you have an idea of these three lifestyles, would you like to find out which style is most like you? Are you going through life as a Navigator, Survivor or a Victim?

It may take a little courage to honestly answer the questions, but your health, vitality and longevity may depend on it. To receive your individualized computerized assessment, go to **www.navigatingforsuccess.com** and click the yellow box that says "Are you a Navigator?" Then, simply answer the questions.

The profile will provide your score along with several areas you might want to work on. You can take a few moments to enhance your health and personal development. Make sure you approach the questionnaire with candid self-awareness. Once you know your situation, you can plan how you want to change your lifestyle and live your extraordinary life.

THE NAVIGATOR'S GUIDE

Directions: Read each statement and choose the answer that most accurately represents your feelings and beliefs. The scoring system is as follows:

5 Strongly agree (S-A)

4 Somewhat agree (SW-A)

3 Neither agree nor disagree (N-A-N-D)

2 Somewhat disagree (SW-D)

1 Strongly disagree (S-D)

	S-A	SW-A	N-A-N-D	SW-D	S-D
I don't wait until events determine my fate. I take the initiative	5	4	3	2	1
I use best practices and rituals to stay focused on what's important to me	5	4	3	2	1
When there are differences of opinion, I express what I think	5	4	3	2	1
I have confidence in my abilities	5	4	3	2	1
I'm not swept away by first impressions	5	4	3	2	1
I take responsibility for what happens in my life	5	4	3	2	1

	S-A	SW-A	N-A-N-D	SW-D	S-D
I'm the captain of my ship	5	4	3	2	1
I bounce back from upsets and quickly get back on track	5	4	3	2	1
I'm confident about my future	5	4	3	2	1
I know my talents and skills	5	4	3	2	1
Others view me as a leader	5	4	3	2	1
I don't take things at face value; I probe and ask questions	5	4	3	2	1
I am able to shrug off self-doubt and negative thinking	5	4	3	2	1
I review my progress to see if my actions are taking me in the right direction	5	4	3	2	1
I control my destiny	5	4	3	2	1
I don't take things personally	5	4	3	2	1
I have clear goals for my future	5	4	3	2	1
I know what I'm passionate about and what really motivates me	5	4	3	2	1
I have a personal vision that is not easily swayed by outside influence	5	4	3	2	1
I'm a good problem solver	5	4	3	2	1
Luck is on my side	5	4	3	2	1

	S-A	SW-A	N-A-N-D	SW-D	S-D
I basically trust people	5	4	3	2	1
I successfully adapt to new situations	5	4	3	2	1
I make plans to accomplish my goals	5	4	3	2	1
I consider the implications or consequences of my actions before I leap into action	5	4	3	2	1
I feel good about life, even when things aren't going well	5	4	3	2	1
I express my feelings when I'm upset	5	4	3	2	1
People have told me that I'm a good listener	5	4	3	2	1
I live my life	5	4	3	2	1
I learn from my mistakes and always keep the end state or goal in mind	5	4	3	2	1
I am clear about my underlying needs, desires and goals	5	4	3	2	1
Life is full of golden opportunities waiting to be discovered	5	4	3	2	1
I don't blame others when things don't work out	5	4	3	2	1
I usually manage my emotions, especially fear and anger	5	4	3	2	1
I am comfortable giving critical feedback to others	5	4	3	2	1

Now, add up your scores from your previous
35 responses: ☐

Navigators usually score between 160 and 175

Survivors usually score between 140 and 159

Victims usually score between 125 and 139

To find out how to improve your score, go to
navigatingforsuccess.com and take the electronic
version of the above questionnaire. At the end, you
will see the root causes of difficulties you might have.

The questionnaire is a fundamental tool, because better
understanding yourself is the first step to developing the
mindset for longevity.

Chapter 7:

CHANGE, RADICAL LIFE EXTENSION AND IMMORTALITY

Ask yourself the following questions:

» Are you a creature of comfort?

» Do you seek out new adventures and opportunities?

» Do you prefer to play it safe?

» Do you prefer to jump in first and figure out the details later?

» Would you rather ask for permission or later ask for forgiveness?

» Are you a *Ready, Aim and Fire* person or a *Ready, Fire and Aim* one?

CHANGE

Some people are attracted to change while others prefer stability and predictability. Whichever one you choose, change is inevitable.

Every day, we are confronted with changes at the personal, physical and social level. Change simply means that something ends and something else begins. While this does not sound like a difficult concept, something about it tends to throw many people into upset and confusion.

PERSONAL CHANGE

Personally, you start life as an infant, grow into early childhood and later morph into adolescence. One day, you are an adorable, bubbly and inquisitive child. Later, you may find yourself as a teenager spending more time alone or immersing yourself in your peer group in a semi-independent manner — neither fish nor fowl; no longer a child, yet not a functioning adult.

Upon graduation from high school, you may leave home and transition to a college experience, further distancing yourself from your home roots. Work follows, as does possibly marriage and having a family.

Each step of the way requires new learning, experimentation and integration. The fact of change does not guarantee success. You have to figure it out along the way. For some, it is an adventure welcomed with anticipation. For others, each change may bring anxiety, confusion and frustration.

Changes can take many forms during the rhythms of a human life.

Once you may have been single, and then you are married.

Once you were married without children, then you have children. To this point, very few seem prepared to parent and the new challenge can be daunting. In fact, this change can take years for one to adapt to the new identity and responsibility.

At some point, your children leave home and you become an empty nester, once again necessitating letting go and learning new skills. It may even take considerable time to relinquish the parenting role and adapt to a life without the responsibility of child rearing.

Throughout our lifespan, the one thing we could always count on throughout has been death. After all, all living things eventually die, right?

According to the second law of thermodynamics, all things experience entropy over time. They wear away, decompose and decay. Ultimately, whether due to biological dynamics, physics, disease, our genetic blueprint or just the wear and tear of life, we are all pulled like a force of gravity into entropy and life terminates.

That has been our destiny since the earliest organisms took form in our evolutionary past and has remained so, at least into the early part of the 21st century.

This death belief, the inevitability of death, an end to life, has become hardwired into our evolutionary memory and nervous system. It is perhaps the most powerful and pervasive human belief — and the one most resistant to change.

Yet, socially and culturally, changes have blasted our sense of stability, order and safety, particularly over the last 25 years. In my case, I remember as a young child visiting my Aunt Gertrude and using her outhouse since she did not have indoor toilets. There once was a time when there was no Internet, smart phones or social media. We communicated either face-to-face, by land line phones or through writing. Today, Facebook, Twitter, Snapchat and other forms of electronic social media have become the major mode of communication and connection, however fleeting and insubstantial at times.

I remember party lines where several households shared the same phone line, slide rules, hand calculations, wind-up watches, and three channels on the TV. Oh, and not color TV but good old, reliable black-and-white. For many older adults, these are ancient times in objective time but close to our hearts in emotional time.

SOCIAL AND CULTURAL

Since the turn of the millennium, change has cascaded upon the world like a tsunami. The rise of terrorism, the destruction of the World Trade Towers and other self-inflicted disasters have tilted the world into a fear-based orientation. Do you remember a time before the TSA, long security lines and taking your shoes off in airports? Now you can't even bring your own bottle of water onboard a commercial flight.

At one time, tragic events were communicated more slowly through newspaper reporting. Today, we see them first hand through instant pictures and videos.

No longer user-friendly, the news is fraught with nightly updates on terroristic attacks, mass killings and other events that dislodge us from feeling safe and secure.

At one time, the common cold was the pain of the day. Today, our suffering is more a matter of post-traumatic stress disorder (PTSD) and chronic anxiety.

Technologically, change has altered the business of how we connect. In 2000, there were 97 million mobile phone subscribers in the U.S. By 2010, this number increased to almost 293 million. In essence, we are a nation marinating in a sea of Wi-Fi.

In 2000, there were zero Facebook users. By 2010, there were 116 million. This has led some researches to state that we are all now linked together by a common electromagnetic nervous system (A. Crouch, 2010).

END OF THE MAJORITY

Cultural majorities are becoming a thing of the past. Many black neighborhoods have been populated by a nearly 50 percent integration of Hispanics. In fact, since the year 2000, thirty million Hispanics have been added to the U.S. population (2014). White rural communities have seen an explosive immigration of Asian and Latin Americans, and by 2030, there is a good chance that white Caucasians might slip into minority status.

Even the venerable Roman Catholic Church has been hit by change and reduction in membership due to the loss of confidence through sexual abuse by priests and the cover-up for decades by its leaders.

Other significant changes are the reductions in people who identify themselves as traditional Evangelical Christians, Republicans or Democrats. There is, in fact, an increased polarization between political parties, a sharp rhetoric of division and an apparent inflexibility to seek common ground. The consensus seems to be a power struggle, one in which blame, character assassinations and distrust form the basis of communication. Whatever happened to the days where Congress and the President seemed to work things out through logical debate, discussion and collaboration?

Traditional sex roles also are changing, even though the resistance to such change is powerful in the more conservative groups. The gay and lesbian movements, along with the growing transgender minority, are altering the dynamics of traditional relationships. Single-sex civil and marital relationships have increased during the last decade. In 2001, the Netherlands was the first county to recognize same sex marriage (CNN, 2001). In 2000, the household norm was one mother and father and two children. Yet, more than a decade later, by 2013, there were more than 250,000 same sex marriages (A. Roberts, 2015).

In addition, in 2000, approximately 19.5 percent of all households were single-parent. Ten years later, by 2010, the percentage of single-parent households increased to almost 30 percent.

Today, four out of 10 children are currently born to unwed mothers.

TIPPING POINT
With these personal, technological, social and cultural changes, we may be at a turning point with regard to change in our country. The shift is so profound that it is difficult to connect our current cultural state to the America of just 10 or 15 years ago.

Indeed, stunning changes are occurring.

THE FUTURE

The most significant changes are still to come. Break-throughs in radical life extension are leading us into a world of scientific and medical advances that will power-fully alter our life paths. Over the next 25 years, advances in biotechnology, nanotechnology, genome therapies, stem cell, 3-D organ and tissue printing, and artificial intelligence will shift the paradigm that has defined lifespan on the planet. Currently, the lifespan is between 78 to 82 years for most people.

According to the U.S Census Department, the number of people living into their 90s grew from 720,000 in 1980 to 1.9 million in 2010. Those people living to age 90 and beyond are the fastest growing group in the older population, according to Richard Suzman, Director of the Division of Behavior and Social Research at the National Institution of Aging (S. Rein erg, 2011). By 2050, their ranks could reach almost 9 million (U.S. Census Bureau, 2011).

An increasing number of Americans are living to age 100. Nationwide, the centenarian population has grown from 32,194 people in 1980 to 53, 364 in 2010 (U.S. Census Bureau, 2011). Worldwide, the numbers are similar. In Japan, the number has quadrupled in the last 10 years, making Japan the most dramatic in terms of life expectancy. By 2050, it is predicted that Japan proportionately will have the most centenarians in the world (S. Goodman, 2016).

While China does not have a high percentage of people over age 100 (only about 7,000 people), the rate of population growth will result in 450,000 centenarians by 2050.

The "official" world's oldest person currently lives in Japan: Yone Minigawa, 114 (S. Goodman, 2011).

When it comes to our "superheroes," that is, those living past their 110th birthday, the "super centenarians," there are estimated to be 300 to 450 living today in the world. The oldest age attained by this group was 115, but this has been surpassed (Anderson, 2012).

In the past, aging occurred incrementally in terms of lifespan. In 1900, life expectancy was around 46 to 48 years. By the year 2000, it had risen to 75 to 82, a sixty percent change (National Statistics Report). As this trend suggests, the dynamics of aging and lifespan are soon to change.

Advances in radical life extension will probably obliterate these past figures and set new norms for the planet. As the diseases of aging are cured, if not aging itself, it is anyone's guess as to how long people will live: 150, 250, 500 years? Maybe we will even achieve immortality.

So, how does a person comprehend and get his hands around this notion of immortality? How is he to envision and picture living to such an age?

What will we look like at age 250?

What role will artificial intelligence and genetic reprogramming play in shaping our physical and mental forms?

Will we look like "Robocop" from the movie: half-human and half-bionic?

Will we speak 20 languages or be masters of any skill we select?

Will we communicate through mental telepathy and only have fond memories of our antique smart phones and electronic social media?

The possibilities are tantalizing and unlimited!

Yet, while scientific and technological thinking and experimentation are pushing through the invisible barrier of Death Psychology and immortality, our psychological and emotional systems still lag far behind. Perhaps the changes required may be too daunting for some?

COPING AND MANAGING EXPONENTIAL CHANGE IN LIFE SPAN

» How will each of us deal with these powerful changes?

» Will you mourn the loss of a simpler and more predictable time?

» Will you embrace change with a sense of adventure and opportunity?

According to William Bridges (1991), most people do not find change easy. They appear to move through four distinct stages, each one requiring a fair degree of navigational control and emotional grounding.

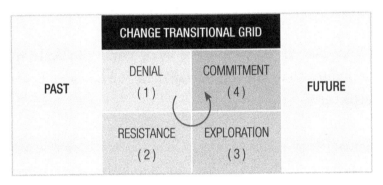

What to Make of the Change Grid and Resiliency Profiles

Taking the Change and Transition Grid and your Resiliency Profiles into account, the greatest difficulty regarding change will be in the Resistance Stage. Survivors and Victims in particular will struggle through this stage in the form of fear, agitation and depression. Not only will they have to contend with a "letting go" of the past when confronted with the reality that their old adaptive and attitudinal attachments may no longer be viable, but they also will struggle with an acceptance of the new realities of radical life extension — that is, figuring out what new models of reality, lifespan and religious beliefs make the most sense.

Many might feel a threat to their religious convictions, especially the more conservative and orthodox followers. After all, for centuries they have been told about the afterlife, the Second Coming, the Rapture of Christ, Heaven and Hell and the promise of everlasting life. They have handed down sacred books, paintings and sculptures with these concepts for generations.

What will the new existence of potential physical immortality do to alter or destroy these fundamental belief structures?

James Strole and his partner, Bernadeanne, describe the experience to that of Chuck Yeager as he became the first person to fly faster than the speed of sound, thus breaking the sound barrier (J Strole et al, 1999).

Yeager confronted an immense vibration, a violent shaking of both the airplane and his body. Rather than slowing down, he increased his flight speed, past the sound threshold, and broke into a world of smooth flying.

Like his flight, change can feel like an intense shaking and vibration, and create fear of moving forward.

For many, slowing down and backing away become the actions of choice, playing it safe. Others increase their speed and push through the Speed of Fear. Perhaps you can relate: are you a change resister or change pursuer?

And what about the enormity for planning to finance a future of 250 or more years of life?

With such a long life, will you have enough money to pay bills and retire?

Will there be such a thing as retirement?

Will people need life or medical insurance?

Is it too selfish for some to consider they are entitled to a healthy life with no significant illnesses to deal with?

And what if some want to opt out and die? Will they be able to do so?

There also may be a fear that the very rich and other elite groups will capitalize on the radical health movement and charge exorbitant fees for the privilege of living a long time.

I think it is a naive hope to think the majority of people are going to jump on the longevity bandwagon and embrace radical life extension.

As limiting as it may be, many might have a stake in keeping things the way they are, especially those in the life, medical and disability insurance businesses. After all, there is a lot of money to be made keeping our medical and drug systems the way they are. It simply is too profitable.

And what about the ultimate death industry: the undertakers, mortuary and burial businesses? Do you think they will go quietly into the night without protest? What benefit will the radical life movement afford these groups and might it be to their advantage to throw obstacles in the way of the revolutionary breakthroughs that will alter our thinking about lifespan?

I raise these questions to help others anticipate and think about the unintended consequences of creating rapid changes without carefully considering the anxieties radical change can provoke.

DENIAL
In the Denial Phase, the person simply does not get what is going on. The message does not get through. He may think:

"Who cares?"
"It isn't happening!"
"It will be over soon!"
"It's a fad!"

RESISTANCE

Once the message gets through, the person has a strong reaction to the change.

There is a high level of stress and reactivity, often resulting in anxiety, anger and rigidity. He may think:

"I am frustrated."
"This makes me angry."
"I'm sad, there is too much to lose if things change."

EXPLORATION

As the resistance is worked through, the person starts to entertain the thought that maybe the change has possibilities. He is not yet committed but is considering available options. You can only deny and resist so long. Maybe, the change could work out. He may think:

"Let me look this over again."
"It seems overwhelming but maybe we can make
it work out."
"Although it isn't what I really want to do, I'll see
what happens."

COMMITMENT

In the final phase of this four-step transition, there is a sense that the vision or new direction makes sense. Clarity is present and actions follow the change initiative. The person is finally on board. He may be thinking:

"This makes sense."

"I finally get it!"

"Let's get into action."

"It's good to get things back to normal again."

HOW PEOPLE EXPERIENCE
THE TRANSITION PROCESS

From a lifestyle perspective, Navigators are best able to transition through these four stages of change. They move through Resistance as soon as possible and begin to explore the essence of the change and next steps. Instead of succumbing to drama and storytelling, they apply their emotional energy toward productive ends. They do not dribble it away by ruminating and holding onto upsets.

They are drawn to explore the vision, experience the change and take advantage of the new opportunity. While some anxiety may naturally exist, they use it to move through the change process. They tend not to flee or fight, but rather to engage and connect with others who may be experiencing similar changes. They develop a vision of where they are going, construct a plan and move into action. Once committed, they become the leaders of change.

On the other hand, Survivors make a lot of noise. With a tendency to fight the change, they likely experience frustration and anger. Rather than getting on with the changes required, they can drift into power struggles. They dig their heels in and defiantly push back.

The good news is that they make their feelings known and, if the change leaders do a good job of listening and getting to the root causes of their resistance, Survivors often shift into exploration mode.

If given sound reasoning, something to be potentially gained and a path to follow, some resisters will try a little exploration. They can't be pushed or they feel controlled and more firmly dig in their heels. They need time. Time to complain, express their fears and examine the costs of remaining stuck.

Victims, too, are different from Navigators. They may feel overwhelmed, throw their hands up in exasperation, complain to each other and become depressed. They either leave the scene or accommodate out of fear. Basically, they feel powerless in response to the change.

Yet, like the chick who perishes within the egg, they can only end up perishing by the changes that surround and ultimately overwhelm them.

WHAT IS YOUR IMMORTALITY CHANGE RESILIENCY QUOTIENT (ICRP)?

Try your hand at the following questionnaire to see how much of a change agent you really are. The questionnaire is not scientifically validated but may offer some insights into where you stand in relation to the coming changes in radical life extension.

YOUR IMMORTALITY CHANGE RESILIENCY PROFILE

Purpose: The ICR Profile was designed to help you identify your outlook on change and immortality. **Directions:** Read each statement and circle your response.

	STRONGLY AGREE	AGREE	NEUTRAL	DISAGREE	STRONGLY DISAGREE
I think the possibility of immortality has many facets and the opportunities are grand	5	4	3	2	1
I expect the world of immortality to have many shifting variables	5	4	3	2	1
I view disruption as a natural phenomenon	5	4	3	2	1
I see major change as uncomfortable but I believe that hidden benefits usually exist	5	4	3	2	1
I believe there are usually important lessons to be learned from radically increasing my lifespan	5	4	3	2	1
I see life as generally rewarding	5	4	3	2	1
I believe I will be able to reestablish my perspective following significant disruption to my mortality beliefs	5	4	3	2	1

	STRONGLY AGREE	AGREE	NEUTRAL	DISAGREE	STRONGLY DISAGREE
I believe the change journey into immortality is a manageable process	5	4	3	2	1
I have a high tolerance for ambiguity	5	4	3	2	1
I need only a brief recovery time from disappointment	5	4	3	2	1
I feel empowered anticipating a change into immortality	5	4	3	2	1
I know my own strengths and weaknesses and can accept my internal and external limits	5	4	3	2	1
I am able to challenge and modify my own assumptions about immortality	5	4	3	2	1
I rely on nurturing relationships for support	5	4	3	2	1
I display patience, insight and humor when thinking about radically extending my lifespan	5	4	3	2	1
I recognize the underlying themes facing me as I journey into immortality	5	4	3	2	1
I am able to organize several unrelated factors into a central theme	5	4	3	2	1
I am able to renegotiate priorities during significant changes	5	4	3	2	1
I can handle many tasks and demands at the same time	5	4	3	2	1
I can compartmentalize stress and self-regulate so I do not get overwhelmed	5	4	3	2	1

YOUR IMMORTALITY CHANGE
RESILIENCY PROFILE

Scoring and interpretation

Add the total of all the numbers you circled.
Enter the total after item 20 here:

If your score is:

| 88-100 | **Navigator Mode** |

You perceive yourself as being highly flexible in change situations involving Immortality and radical life extension.

| 76-87 |

You perceive yourself as being relatively flexible with regard to Immortality and change.

| 64-75 | **Survivor Mode** |

You perceive yourself as being flexible in some aspects of change and Immortality. Depending on your existing state and the nature of the change, you may or may not find change comfortable.

| 52-63 |

You perceive yourself as being relatively inflexible in response to Immortality and change. You tend to hang on to established ways of doing things until you see the value of change.

Below 52	Victim Mode

Victim Mode

You perceive yourself as being very inflexible in response to Immortality and change. You may feel helpless or victimized when faced with change. Your personal resources for adjusting to change are easily drained.

In summary, change can be difficult and scary. The future holds great promise for radical life extension and immortality in whatever form it might take. It will, perhaps, be the most monumental change in human history, one that will require considerable courage and vision to transcend our evolutionary legacy of Death Psychology and incremental changes. How might you move into the new world that beckons?

It is coming.

We just have to choose whether or not we engage it as Navigators, Survivors or Victims.

If Breakthrough Thinking and Navigation lifestyle appeal to you, see if you can answer these six important questions about vision, purpose, identity and skills.

» Where am I going?

» What do I want?

» Why do I want this?

» Why is it important to me?

» Who do I have to be to get there?

» What tools and skills do I need to learn to succeed?

Your answers will go a long way in laying a foundation for your change journey, providing a GPS to keep you out of emotional drama and guiding you on your path.

Chapter 8:

YOUR BRAIN HOLDS THE KEY

Now that you have a basic understanding of how people journey through life and an understanding of your personal style as a Navigator, Survivor or Victim, you may want to learn how to shift into the way of living life as a Navigator. After all, Navigators seem to have more fun, are more successful, are in better health and are satisfied with their lives (Jackson, 2010).

Realizing that every day they can engage life as either an investment or a cost, they work to maximize their return on investment in their lives. Everyone has certain resources they can use to enhance the quality of their lives: time, energy, money and intelligence. In a later chapter, we will examine how Navigators use these resources to break out of anxious living into the domain of extraordinary living.

Right now, let's look at how our brains are wired and how we can better use this powerful resource to enhance our lives and prolong our life, energy and vitality.

THE BRAIN

The brain is our most versatile organ. It exists to serve us and move us into action. But, to use your brain as effectively as Navigators, there are some essential facts you must know.

Consisting of 100 billion neurons, the brain works 24/7 to keep us alive and safe. Weighing only about three pounds, it consists of mostly gray matter, the composition of tofu. Yet, this marvelous organ controls all of our bodily and mental functions.

No brain means no body or mental life!

Every neuron has multiple connections to other neurons and linkages to every cell in the body. Within this immense neural network, each neuron fires energetic impulses 5 to 50 times a second. In a single second, then, there are approximately 20 million billion firings, shooting off to keep us erect, breathing, heart pumping, digesting, our muscles strong, balance intact, thoughtful and responsive to our environment. These neurons communicate through signals of information into the nervous system, in a constant flow of information. This information management is what the brain does.

The mind could be said to do the work of the brain, enabling action and engagement in the world. The brain creates the mind, which interacts with the structural brain and impacts its form and function.

No one knows how the brain makes the mind or how the mind uses the brain, especially in conscious experiencing such as relating to others, envisioning, dreaming, developing personality, managing stress or throwing a ball. The brain is part of a tangible, visible and measurable world in our bodies. Mind is part of the invisible world of thoughts, feelings, attitudes, beliefs and imagination. The mind is not confined to the brain, yet appears to permeate to every cell throughout the body.

According to Dan Siegel, our minds are created within relationships — including the one that we have with ourselves. Each of us has a unique mind.

The brain is highly responsive to how we treat it and different parts of the brain are responsible for different functions. It is very flexible and neuroplastic. In other words, although it is ensconced in your skull and can't be directly touched, it can be modified and redesigned as a function of your inputs, such as nutrition, emotions and your thinking mind.

To take advantage of this neuroplasticity, we must first appreciate the fact that we actually have three functionally interconnected brains instead of one. According to Paul MacLean (1990), a neuroscientist, a useful model is to think of the brain as a Triune Brain, a three-part system that has evolved throughout time.

Our neocortex and our frontal lobes make up the youngest and newest member of the brain.

The second brain is the emotional brain, the limbic system.

The third is the reptilian, the survival brain.

One way to simplify and grasp how these three brains operate is to think of them as your Computer Brain, Gorilla Brain and Alligator Brain.

THE COMPUTER BRAIN
The youngest brain is the Computer Brain, located behind the forehead. It is almost 75,000 years old. Pretty old, you might surmise!

The Computer Brain works to help us figure things out, solve problems and create order. This area is the seat of goal-setting and vision creation.

Also the center for learning, it appears to rapidly develop after the age of seven. As the home of logic and intellect, it strives to help us "cool down" and understand what is going on around us. Its messages, in response to emotional upset, are: "Don't be aggressive," "Think before you act" and "Don't be loud!"

Although it tries to manage emotions, it struggles with its more powerful neighbors, the Gorilla and Alligator Brains.

THE GORILLA BRAIN

The Gorilla Brain resides in the limbic area, the middle part of our brain. Originating nearly one million years ago, it is considerably older than its neighbor, the Computer Brain. As our mammalian brain, the Gorilla is powerfully present from age one to five. It is the home of our emotions and values, hosting little thought but a whole lot of feeling. As our primary worry center, it can shift between very contradictory and confusing feelings. For example, feelings of love one moment can transform quickly to anger or hate the next.

Sometimes, the Gorilla Brain can team up with its youthful counterpart, the Computer, to guide emotional upset toward successful action. It seeks pleasure, avoids pain and exhibits a tremendous appetite for bonding or attachment to others. If attachment during the early years is inconsistent or insecure, it does not bode well for successful relationships later in life.

By "secure attachment," I refer to parent-child relationships that are based on a caring, reliable and consistent care-taking adult who serves to create a safe home environment for the growing child.

When parent-child relationships are unpredictable, blow alternately hot and cold, exhibit tension and anger, insecurity becomes more the household climate, resulting in feelings of danger and distrust. Often, children growing up in such anxious environments find it difficult to form safe and secure adult relationships. The early damage to trust and predictability may seem too overwhelming for the emerging adult to overcome on his own.

THE ALLIGATOR BRAIN

The third brain is the Alligator, the Reptilian part. It is the oldest brain, going back almost 400 million years! Residing at the base of the skull in the region of our basal ganglia, it conducts basic housekeeping functions such as regulating our breathing, sleep, heartbeat and other vital processes. Its focus is survival, protection and procreation. While it is not smart or inventive like the Computer Brain, it is consistent in applying its own brand of reptilian intelligence. It responds to threats in a "fight or flight" manner. Although not very sophisticated, it nevertheless is effective in being vigilant to danger 24/7. Some refer to the Alligator as our instinctive brain.

The Alligator does not trust the Computer or Gorilla for one simple fact. If danger is really present and these two neighbors cannot successfully and quickly reduce its presence, the person could be in danger of severe injury or death. Therefore, in dangerous situations, the Alligator rises in full power to take charge and ensure our safety. It does not mind being wrong. On the contrary, it thinks, "Better safe than sorry," because death is an unacceptable outcome.

Here's an example. Imagine that you are out for a stroll in the forest. On the trail, you see what looks like a curved stick. Your Gorilla Brain says, "Pick it up and use it as a walking stick!" or "Have some fun with it and make believe it is a sword."

But your Alligator screams, "No, leave it there! It could be a poisonous snake!"

In response, your heart rate quickens and you become short of breath. You decide to take a step back and seek another trail to walk. Perhaps that attractive stick was really a poisonous snake. Your Alligator takes pride that it probably protected you from a painful and potentially lethal bite.

WHICH BRAIN WINS?

So, if there is a choice of action, which brain wins? Often, especially under threat, the Alligator prevails. It does not want change or any type of disruption. Instead, it craves certainty and comfort. As a product of hundreds of millions of years of evolutionary development, it has learned to instinctively avoid fear and danger.

The Alligator connects fear with the anticipation of future pain. Any new action such as changing jobs or leaving a relationship can become problematic and stressful.

Usually disruptive and unpredictable, change can trigger a sense of anxiety or potential danger. When these feelings arise, the survival brain anticipates the worst, springing instinctively into a fight or flight reaction pattern. Any further change may portend catastrophe.

Even though these actions are not intrinsically dangerous, your reptilian brain does not want to take the risk. To the Alligator, it just might be a poisonous snake. With no interest in being creative or experimental, the Alligator Brain is reactive, existing only to keep us safe. And given the 2,000 negative thoughts and 50 or so stress points we consciously experience each day, it works hard to protect us from all the dangers that might impair our well-being.

The ultimate task for each of us is to first appreciate how these three brains function and then to figure out how to create an integrated neighborhood where the Computer, Gorilla and Alligator can work together for our success and longevity. If that were possible, there would be less inter-brain competition, mistrust and internal conflict. Consequently, the harmful hormones of cortisol and adrenaline would be reduced and we would experience greater peace of mind, control and contentment. This could translate into a reduced risk of internal inflammation and organic breakdown.

The Navigator, more than the Survivor or Victim, probably has the greatest likelihood of discovering the secret to the brain puzzle.

Now let's examine what forces make such collaboration difficult to achieve. We'll look at the prevalent tendency for most of us to stay stuck in the Victim and Survivor identities and feel predestined to anxiety and misery.

Key Points

- The brain exists to move us into action.

- Our total brain consists of three parts, each having evolved over time: the Neocortex, the Limbic System and the Survival Brain.

- A simple way to understand our three brains is to think of the Neocortex as our Computer, the Limbic System as our Gorilla, and the Survival Brain as our Alligator.

- The Computer seeks to ruminate and solve problems. The Gorilla wants to feel good, eliminate pain and experience great relationships. The Alligator wants safety and to stay alive.

- While these three brains are in competition with each other, the Alligator usually emerges victorious.

- The brain is capable of change through neuroplasticity.

- Navigators are best suited to creating an environment of cooperation and collaboration between the three competitors. They do this through self-awareness, emotional regulation, learning and constantly reprogramming the brain.

• —— | • | • | • | —— •

Chapter 9:

| LIFE SUCKS!

Navigational living has to be learned but, truthfully, the cards seem to be stacked against us.

First, because of the dominant evolutionary history of the Alligator Brain, our brain is wired more for anxiety than happiness. Although designed to keep us safe and protect us, the Alligator does so with an interesting side effect — that is, leaving us feeling anxious and scared much of the time.

Unfortunately, our Computer Brain has not evolved to a stage of consistently evaluating if our fear is real. It also could do a better job in reducing our fear response more quickly, thus minimizing the corresponding secretions of adrenaline and cortisol.

One would hope that after 400 million years, the oldest part of our brain might be more secure and thriving. Unfortunately, this is not the case. The Alligator Brain has evolved to be expert at avoiding danger. According to the Alligator in each of us, our fear is what keeps us alive.

Better to be afraid and alive than happy and dead.

Always vigilant, the Alligator is constantly aware of potential threats. Its sole duty is to be our sentry, our guardian at the gate. Its eternal task is to take care of us, even at the cost of our emotional distress.

So what are the sources of stress in our lives that necessitate such concern?

Well, consider all the times we fret about things on a daily basis.

Humans seem to have a vast treasure of things to worry about, things both real and imagined.

We worry about tax audits, getting bitten by a dog, dealing with certain difficult people at work, things people say to us, how our kids are doing, an upcoming doctor's appointment, making a presentation to a group or team, asking for a raise, asking someone out on a date, paying bills, saving for retirement, and even what to wear to a party.

TEENAGE WORRIES
Adults are not the only chronic worriers. Teenagers are plagued with worries as well. Among other things, they are anxious about social rejections, being teased or bullied, acting cowardly, their appearance, being picked

last for a team, sounding stupid, and disappointing their parents and teachers.

Adding the stress of SATs and college applications or lacking a vision or direction for their future career, their anxieties could reach the level of terror and panic. According to research findings at TTI, a testing company that assesses behavior, values and competence, the two greatest cognitive weaknesses for many college graduates are visionary thinking and decision-making, the two key skills of Navigational thinking (Bonnstader, 2009).

CHILDHOOD WORRIES
Are children immune from worrying? Unfortunately not! Children have wild imaginations that create fantastical fears like being kidnapped, burglars in the house, and boogey men in the closet.

In fact, boogeymen in the closet were one of my greatest fears. As soon as the bedroom light went off, I could sense their presence, waiting for the right moment to pounce and attack me as I slept. My mother, more worried about the cost of electricity, would not allow me to keep the light on in the closet, which was the one force that boogeymen detested.

Consequently, I spent several years of my childhood sleeping with a flashlight, baseball bat and Swiss army knife.

My mother finally relented and let me keep the light on. It was only due to the fact that at the age of six, I broke her nose when she came into my darkened room one night. Thinking she was the boogeyman from my closet, I lashed out to protect myself when she leaned over me. After that regrettable incident, she never said a word about turning my closet light off ever again.

Children also worry about real life issues such as their parents divorcing, not having friends, being teased or bullied, neighborhood violence, and school shootings. The media does nothing to help children's worries. Here is an interesting statistic: by the time a child is eight years old, he will have seen almost 8,000 deaths by gunshot on TV.

On a more global level, we are frequently besieged by terrible, anxiety-producing news. Over the time period beginning with the horrific shootings at Sandy Hook Elementary School in 2012 to the end of year 2015, there have been more than 90,000 deaths by gunshot in the United States.

Also, the political landscape is marred by a language of hysteria and paranoia which taps directly into the scared Survivor Brain.

Rogue nations like North Korea and terrorist organizations like ISIS are priming for nuclear warfare or looking to invade our homeland. To top it off, we are bombarded with hysterical rhetoric, anxiety and xenophobia by people trying to convince us that immigrants are trying to take our country away from us.

Politicians espouse mass deportations and building massive walls to keep "the barbarians" out.

And don't forget about global warming and the impending massive hurricanes, floods, food shortages and general pandemonium.

Are you worried yet?

THE MEDIA
The bottom line to both our personal worries and the threats from others can be overwhelming, especially to our overworked and not very smart Alligator Brain. How is this primitive sentry to determine the real from the imagined, from direct danger to hysterical fantasizing?

Every day we wake up to the threat of potential disasters and the fear that no one is in control. For example, here are the headlines from one day's newspaper coverage in 2013. On February 2, 2013, the *New York Times* bombarded us with the following:

"Swollen with Syrian Refugees, Lebanon Feels its Stitching Fray"

"Fault-Finding Grows as Cuts Near"

"Major Banks Aid in Payday Loans Banned by States and Interest Can Top 500 Percent"

"North Korea Threatens U.S. Over Joint Military Drill"

"Make Your Neighbors Envy You"

"With Economy Floundering, Apathy Grips Voters in Cypress"

"Angry and Disillusioned, Italians Prepare to Vote"

"Seen as Nature Lover's Paradise, Utah Struggles with Air Quality"

"Emory University's Leader Reopens its Racial Wounds"

"Fault-Finding in Washington Grows Intense Over Sequestration"

Here are some 2016 headlines I came across in a recent Sunday *New York Times*:

"Pentagon Details Chain of Errors in Afghan Strike," about the disastrous mistaken destruction of a Doctors Without Borders hospital that killed 42 people.

"As Attacks Surge, Boys & Girls Fill Israeli Jails," describing a surge in Palestinian minors incarcerated for a wave of violence that has killed more than 30 Israelis in seven months.

"'Sincerely Sorry,' Ex-Auschwitz Guard Says at Trial" speaks for itself.

"Refugee Dies After Self-Immolation in Protest of Australian Policy" — toward migrants trying to reach its shores.

"Cruz, in Indiana, Attacks Trump for Supporting Transgender Rights." God forbid we should reach a level of compassion and generosity instead of religious fanaticism.

"Deals Elude Congress, Where Little is Bi-Partisan Besides Distrust & Blame." Great modelling, don't you think, to teach our children the democratic way?

"Mocking Critics, Trump Says Unity Isn't Necessary"

"Arizona Scorpions Get an Early Start On Summer!" Check your kids' shoes before they put their feet in them!

There is more, but you get the point.

IS ANYONE IN CONTROL?

How do you feel after reading those gems? Calm and optimistic for the future? Safe and secure about our leaders and government?

I think not.

On a daily basis, we are flooded with real and imagined threats that bombard our senses and overwhelm our ability to put things in perspective. This leads us to feeling that we have little, if any, control over our lives. As I mentioned earlier, 80 percent of our daily 2,500 conscious thoughts are negative.

And 90 percent of the time, we repeat the same thoughts the next day, like in the movie *Groundhog Day*.

What else can our lonely and vigilant Alligator Brain do but keep us on high alert to all those snakes on our path?

We remain marinated in our own anxiety juices of adrenaline and cortisol, a deadly cocktail that eats away at our soft tissue and causes chronic inflammation and physical breakdown, thus potentially shortening our lifespan.

As Ray Kurzweil and Terry Grossman (2009) so aptly put it in their book *Transcend: Nine Steps to Living Well Forever*, "There's no way around it, life is stressful."

At all levels — evolutionary, developmental, global, local and personal — we are constantly bombarded by worrisome issues and thoughts. No one is immune.

At an earlier time in human history, stress may have operated better in terms of survival. After all, those ancestors who survived animal predators passed on certain genes to the next generations. Our physical body and its multiple systems have evolved to help us survive life-and-death situations by masterfully designing our fight or flight reaction system.

When in a perceived or real danger that demands a quick survival reaction and a burst of physical exertion, the fight or flight response was an elegant solution.

Once action was taken, expending the adrenaline, noradrenaline and cortisol released from the adrenal glands, the individual could return to a more parasympathetic state of reduced blood pressure, decreased sugar level, heart rate and respiration, along with reduced cholesterol levels. In other words, emergency reactions were soon followed by a relaxation response (H. Benson, 1974).

In modern times, there are not many instances of predatory animals stalking our families and looking for a tasty meal, but our response to perceived stress and danger is still how our survival brains keep us safe. Whether it is heavy traffic, waiting in line, a romantic disappointment, a job interview, or countless other situations, we are constantly engaged in a chronic stimulation of the fight or flight response without the physical release that precedes the relaxation response.

The result of this evolutionary and genetic anomaly is that we are stuck with a certain toxic physiological pathology. Due to these mundane and predictable stressors, we can be left with an unnecessarily high heart rate and blood pressure, thereby triggering bloodstream turbulence and arterial wall tension.

Chronic stress contributes to decreased immunological health, heart disease, gastro-intestinal disorders, Type II diabetes, stroke and cancer. Longevity researchers like Kurzweil strongly point to the impact that chronic stress has on accelerating the aging and death process.

Is there any hope for us struggling humans? It seems like we are doomed to a life of Survivor or Victimhood.

Is there any relief we can bring to our taxed and skittish Alligator Brain?

Does life just suck?

Key Points

- We can learn how to live as a Navigator.
  We are not born that way.

- Stresses in our daily lives are as abundant
  as dust. They never seem to really go away.

- Adults, teenagers and children all suffer from
  anxiety. There is no real complete freedom
  from it.

- It is almost impossible to feel persistent
  calmness and peace of mind.

- Our Alligator Brain is overworked.

- The Alligator Brain does not trust its neighbors,
  the Gorilla and Computer Brains, to work
  together.

- You can learn to rewire your chronically stressed
  brain through self-awareness, self-regulation
  and reprogramming. You can change the genetic
  legacy with which you were born and learn
  to create functional brain integration.

Chapter 10:

THOUGHTS ARE PHYSICAL

Given the daily volume of stressors that intrude on our peace of mind, how do most people deal with life?

As a therapist and coach, I get to hear firsthand about how people cope and self-regulate their emotions. Forty years of practice has led me to conclude that most people seem to cope and deal with problems better than they self-regulate their emotional upsets.

While they basically muddle through most of the problems and frustrations that come their way, they are frequently left with heavy doses of distress, worry and anger. Rather than just deal with an issue and move on, they continue to mull it over and find fault either with themselves or someone else.

Most people take innocent acts personally, as if the other person intended to do harm or take advantage of them. It is as if our minds are Velcro, sticking to upsets and irritations rather than just letting them move along with more of a Teflon protective screen (Hanson, 2013).

NATURE OF AN UPSET

Imagine how you feel when someone cuts you off on the road. You swerve to avoid the oncoming car. As they speed away, you're left feeling breathless, heart racing, with an inner and explosive anger.

You likely will fume over his bad and inconsiderate driving behavior and continue repeating the transgression over and over in your head:

That low-life shmuck! I can't believe what he just did. He could have killed me!

People like that shouldn't be allowed to drive.

Where is a darn cop when you need one?

He didn't even stop or gesture to say he was sorry.

I hope I can catch up with him. I'll show him.

I'll tailgate him and scare him silly.

Your heart may pound and some sweat appears on your palms. In the meantime, the other driver is now miles ahead of you, thinking about the terrific day ahead.

YOUR EMOTIONAL MEMORIES

Because our brain and memories are linked by conceptual and emotional associations, called your emotional memory, then you begin to remember other times you were taken advantage of or treated unfairly.

In a flash, you remember in rapid sequence a recent time you were not called on even though you held your hand up for most of a meeting. A date someone canceled at the last moment. An overcharge on a bill that the company's help desk has ignored but continues to bill you a monthly interest. The time you never got to play on the varsity team and spent the season on the bench.

This causes you to become even more upset, feeling like a victim who has little control over his destiny.

After listing all the things that are wrong or have happened in your life, you think, "Why me? Why do I have to deal with so much?"

» How often do you hear yourself talking to yourself?

» Are you aware of all the negative comments you make to yourself when things don't go your way?

» Do you tend to take things personally and make up stories about how no one really cares about you?

» Do you work yourself up into frustration, anxiety and resentment even after the situation has passed?

» Do any of these following comments fit how you think when frustrated or disappointed?:

Why does this have to happen to me?

It's not fair. He shouldn't be able to get away with that!

What if I didn't swerve? What could have happened to me? I could have been killed.

Life sucks and I'm sick and tired of being pushed around. I'll show them. They will get their due because what goes around comes around.

Sounds a bit like Victim thinking, don't you think?

THOUGHTS CAUSE EMOTIONAL DAMAGE

These kinds of thoughts are not passive. They cause us real emotional and physical harm. Your thoughts trigger emotions which, in turn, trigger physical and chemical reactions. When you think about being taken advantage of and make up a tragic story about how no one cares about you, you might feel saddened, frustrated or angry. These negative thoughts are like photons of energy that smash through your nervous system and elicit the release of adrenaline and cortisol — the chemicals that prepare you for action and defense (B. Lipton, 2005).

Your Survival or Reptilian Brain interprets your thoughts as meaning you are in trouble and quickly begins to mobilize you to either fight back or to flee. The greater the level of personal upset, the more your conscious thinking and problem-solving abilities suffer. As upset rises, cognitive clarity diminishes. In other words, when you feel stressed out or angry, it is hard to think clearly and remain objective. Some researchers and practitioners estimate a person can lose up to 50 percent of his executive thinking under such stress conditions.

TAKING THINGS TOO PERSONALLY

It's easier to take things personally, become dramatic and catastrophize your situation than to stay calm. When you fall into the trap of your thought patterns creating bigger problems for you, you feel emotionally off center. Your body overheats and you are prone to making poor decisions.

Consequently, you now behave or react in such a way to cause a corresponding defensive reaction in the other person. Your reactive behavior pushes the other person to behave rudely in response so that you are now dealing with the anger, negativity and dismissiveness that you first assumed to be true.

Your thinking patterns create a self-fulfilling prophecy. Given the other person's reactions, you have succeeded in proving you were right all along. This results in disconnect, mutual annoyance and a power struggle where the two of you are trying to prove who is really right.

The result of this process is that you have just intensified your pain, created an emotional disconnect and are dealing with secondary difficulties from what you triggered in the other person through your provoking behaviors.

Is there any hope for us struggling humans? We seem to do a really good job at misreading and overreacting to situations that do not, on the surface, go our way.

How easy it is to find blame in someone else for our own personal misery. It sure seems like we are doomed to a life of Victims or Survivors.

Is there any relief we can bring to our struggling Alligator Brain?

Key Points

- People are better able to cope and problem-solve than self-regulate.

- Once triggered by a stress experience, we can marinate in the upsetting feelings for long periods of time.

- Other emotional memories of pain and upset can travel with great speed and force from our past and smash into our present experience, thus yanking us back into useless hurt and emotional traumas.

- It is almost impossible not to take things personally.

- Thoughts are physical and cause emotional reactions.

- When upsets hit us, we can lose perspective and overheat. Once overheated, reactive and poor judgment follows.

- Many of us suck at putting our stresses in perspective and can do a better job at learning how to regulate our stress reactions.

Chapter 11:

THE POWER OF BELIEF

In previous chapters, we explored how the brain is wired for worry and negativity. According to the researchers Bruce Lipton, Rick Hansen, Joe Dispenza and Rob Williams, worry and anxiety are dangerous for our health, well-being and longevity.

As mentioned previously, we experience approximately 60,000 thoughts a day, 80 percent of which are negative. Of this vast amount, our conscious minds are only aware of 2,500 of them.

Again, 80 percent of our thoughts or 2,000 are negative.

"It seems a bit unfair, don't you think — that for every one positive thought we have, there are four negative ones?" In his book, *Hardwiring Happiness: The New Brain Science of Contentment, Calm and Confidence* (2009), Rick Hansen writes about the hidden power of everyday experiences to change your brain and life for the better.

Hansen likens our mind, the brain in action, to a garden of weeds and flowers. To enhance your quality of life, you need to do two things: pull your weeds and nurture your flowers. Your worries and negative thoughts are the weeds, while your positive thoughts, feelings of gratitude and take-charge actions are your flowers.

The mental qualities of appreciation, compassion, humor, perspective taking and vitality do not spring into action on their own. Build these qualities into your neural networks and pathways and a new biology of experience will evolve. You will not have to wait until evolution and genetics create this powerful state of being. We have already waited almost 400 million years without much progress. We can use the neuroplasticity of our brains and epigenesis, the impact of experience and thoughts on our evolving brains, to change our destinies.

NEURAL PLASTICITY
Several studies support the evidence of neural plasticity. In one, Ellen Langer, a Harvard psychologist, explored the power of experience on aging. Eight men 70 years or older stayed in a physical environment where vintage 1959 radio recordings and TV shows were played, along with books and magazines from the same era.

Measurements of physical dexterity, grip strength, flexibility, hearing, vision, memory and cognition, all bookmarkers of age, were taken before and after the study. Results indicated that the experimental group out-performed the control group.

Langer concluded the "men had put their minds in an earlier time and their bodies went along with the ride" (Langer, 2009). The study was replicated in 2010 with similar results, indicating that changes in one's perception of time can lead to physical and mental de-aging.

The implication of this and Langer's original study are that health and illness are deeply rooted in our minds and hearts. How we experience ourselves in the world impacts us more significantly than our usual medical and physical models suggest.

Cole (Dobbs, 2013) writes that the evidence suggests that belief is a powerful determinant of gene expression and behavior. We are the architects of our experiences. Your subjective experience carries more impact than your objective situation.

In other words, your belief carries more weight than your reality.

THE POWER OF MIND

The mind has power. All physical reality is made up of vibrations of energy. Your thoughts are energy vibrations. Consequently, thoughts are powerful influencers and affect what happens to you. Most people probably take little notice of their thinking or how their mind moves, reads, fears, avoids, or what it says to itself.

Your mind power is directing your thoughts toward desired outcomes. What it focuses on, you attract. Focus on fear, then fearfulness will come. Focus on success and you will attract it. What you think about and focus on functions like a telescope, bringing into powerful consciousness the object of your thinking and consideration.

How you use your mind is the cause of suffering. Your mind is a creature of habit. As you train it, it takes on the power to use you. Changes to your internal beliefs and thoughts result in changes to your external conditions. Change your mind; change your life.

According to John Kehoe, just as water takes the shape of its container, so does your mind create and manifest according to the images about which you habitually think. Your subconscious mind continually interprets and acts upon your predominant thoughts. Its mission is to attract circumstances and situations that match the external images.

An analogy is: plant kernels of corn and corn will grow. Your subconscious mind is the fertile ground in which your thought seeds take hold and grow. The subconscious mind does not actually choose these thought seeds. It just absorbs them through your thought and feeling repetition. Once planted, our thoughts seek expression in our lives.

Life Navigators appreciate the power of beliefs and thoughts. They realize that their minds are like transmitters and that every thought has a specific vibration.

Positive thoughts and beliefs have a high vibrational frequency, while negative thoughts such as "I hate you" possess a lower vibration.

If you keep thinking the world is a terrible place, you will see and attract people and experiences that support your notion.

Navigators know that vibrations can shift. You are not Victims at the mercy of your thoughts. You have the power to choose your thoughts, thereby changing your vibrational frequencies and life experiences.

THOUGHTS ARE PHYSICAL

Bruce Lipton writes that thoughts are physical and directly impact our neural wiring and structures. Our fundamental beliefs, whatever they may be, control our thinking. They become the lenses through which we perceive and understand our world.

If you believe, for example, that you are not lovable, you are likely to perceive and interpret rejection or disapproval where they do not exist.

For instance, say someone does not return your call and you jump to the conclusion that the other person does not like you or is angry at you. This negative thinking triggers a chemical reaction and sympathetic nervous system arousal. Immediately, you become upset, hurt and angry. At the speed of light, one hundred trillion cells are bathed in stress-related chemicals, causing your body to feel terrible.

Chances are that the next opportunity you have to interact with this person, you will display an attitude or physical look that expresses displeasure or annoyance. Your thoughts are physical shots of energy. They generate electromagnetic fields that can trigger the other person's mirror neurons to elicit a similar negative emotional reaction even though no words have been spoken.

This emotional exchange happens even though the other person has probably forgotten or does not realize he did not return your call. He picks up your anger and blame through your thoughts.

Remember, thoughts are energy.

Your energy field is activating his energy field like a radio receiver picking up a transmitted message. He then reacts defensively by avoiding you and sending you back a hostile look. Either way, spoken or not, your negative belief has unleashed a bad state of affairs. His reactions then confirm your long-standing belief that you are indeed unlovable.

Hanson, Dispenza, Lipton and Williams would all probably agree that if you keep your mind activated on thinking badly about others, blaming or self-criticisms, your brain will be directed into greater reactivity, susceptibility to depression and anxiety, loss of perspective and rampaging Alligator reactions. When you think in negative terms, you feel emotionally negative. Feel negative for long enough and you create a state of negativity that becomes part of your personality.

Welcome to the prison of suffering you have created through your belief structure.

REFRAMING
If, on the other hand, you can reframe the phone incident and shape a more positive interpretation, your brain will rewire differently.

You could consider that the other person was busy, got distracted or was stressed out. You might even feel some concern or compassion for him. Imagine his surprise and possible delight if you were to then leave a message the next day such as the following: "Sorry we did not connect yesterday. Not sure if you got my message; I didn't hear back from you and got concerned. I hope everything is okay and that there is no emergency. When you get a chance, give me a call so we can connect. I also have some information I want to run by you."

The Emotional or Gorilla Brain, instead of reacting with alarm, fear or annoyance, will probably feel cared for and supported. The Computer Brain gets the message and returns your call. Navigation in action.

If you keep your focus on being less reactive and creating positive experiences, your brain will take a different shape, one with greater resilience, strength and compassion hardwired into it.

Reframing is a powerful cognitive tool to create reality maps that allow people to assess, explore options and navigate workable solutions and mutually satisfying relationships. If, however, the level of emotional reactivity provokes a fear or panic response, it becomes difficult to "stop, look and listen" in order to reflect on several different frames of reference regarding a problematic incident.

In such a case, conceptual thinking becomes impaired and the coping options become severely limited. The best recourse in such situations, if there is enough self-awareness, is to pause, take a time out and regain some measure of safety and perspective. Once calmed down, reframing is more possible.

If you are able to reframe more often, this will likely have a positive effect on your longevity goals.

WHAT ARE YOU PAYING ATTENTION TO?

» What do you pay attention to?

» What are your beliefs?

» Are you creating and prolonging pain, worry and misery through your limiting beliefs, or are you generating a life worth living by building neural networks and pathways that support a powerful, optimistic and healthier life outlook?

Your beliefs create your destiny!

Change your beliefs and rewire your brain.

Rewire your brain and master your destiny.

Rewiring your brain is essential for living into an immortal experience. New beliefs will be essential in helping people escape the gravitational pull of their Death Psychology and propensity to overreact, think the worst and live in Survivor mode.

We will revisit these ideas in more detail in later chapters.

Let's first look at how movies work, in terms of how our beliefs, thoughts and stories create our personal dramas and histories.

Key Points

- Worrying and anxiety are dangerous to our physical health and longevity goals.

- We can change our brains for the better or worse. It is our choice. We have control.

- Changes in time perception and life-enhancing experiences can alter our aging process.

- Belief is more powerful than reality in shaping who we are.

- Change your belief; change your reality.

- What you focus on is what you attract.

- Navigators are continually adjusting and reprogramming their minds through learning, risk-taking, making mistakes and reality tearing. They control their minds while Victims are controlled by their minds.

Chapter 12:

DO YOU LIKE THE MOVIES?

I love going to the movies. I find the whole package wonderful. The smell of buttery popcorn. The sense of excitement. The knowledge that for the next two hours I am going to become enthralled by the magic of film.

I remember one particular time when my wife and two young daughters went to see *Jurassic Park*. In one scene, a character was about to be gobbled up by the escaped and rampaging T-Rex. My wife covered her eyes to avoid watching the torment that was in seconds to be displayed on the screen. My daughter, Laura, who was about eight years old at the time, leaned toward her and whispered, "Mom, it's only a movie!"

As hypnotic devices, movies are designed to deceive us. The truth is that we want to be deceived. That is part of the movie experience: getting lost in the narrative and losing track of our usual reality.

In actuality, there is no real motion picture up there on the screen. A movie consists of hundreds of still shots strung together in a sequence, then fed into a projector that runs the scenes fast enough that they appear to be seamlessly attached.

The movie is being flashed or projected onto the screen. The audience quickly loses track of its origin. Who cares about the guy in the projection room who is creating this magical experience for us? We are here to be entranced.

You might be surprised at how the concept of movies — and our own ability to think and imagine our own reality — play an important role in our overall health and longevity.

YOUR MIND AS A MOVIE PROJECTOR

The human mind and its main function, thinking, mimics a movie projector.

The mind creates thousands of impressions without pause, giving each of us an experience that we recognize as our reality. What we experience in our conversations and activities is all a projection of our varied thoughts onto our world of experience. In fact, nearly 60,000 thoughts flow like a film through our minds every day. Although many of us replay the same mental movie one day after the next, we probably have the experience that something is impacting us from our environment.

In fact, our reality is largely internal and we project it to the screen called life.

Now, some important questions:

» If your life were a movie, what kind would it be?

» Are you living life as an adventure, tragedy or a comedy?

» How about a soap opera or a horror movie?

Would it be such a shock for you to know that your reality is a projection of your internal film: your perceptions, interpretations and emotions?

Many scientists consider your thoughts as the cause of all your feelings and reality. In fact, some have suggested that your thoughts are powerful electromagnetic fields that exert a direct influence over the quality of your life. That means that even if you do not speak them out loud, your thoughts have power.

Masaru Emoto, a Japanese scientist, has conducted some fascinating experiments regarding the power of thoughts. Other scientists have done likewise, but for me, Emoto's work stands out. In his work, Emoto studied the impact of positive and loving thoughts as compared to negative and hateful thoughts on water.

After a person spoke a loving thought to a container of water, Emoto froze the liquid and took microscopic images of its crystallized form.

Loving expressions such as, "I love you" or "Thank you for the health you are giving me," resulted in images of beautiful, geometrically balanced crystals.

On the other hand, negative expressions such as, "You disgust me" or "You fool," gave rise to distorted and grotesque crystals.

In other words, the thoughts that had been expressed actually produced physical changes on the water samples.

YOU ARE YOUR OWN SCRIPT WRITER

Generalizing from these studies, you might consider the impact your thinking — redundant, negative movie is having on your own container of water — your body. After all, each of us is made up of around 65 percent water.

If your movie is a horror story, what might it be doing to your internal cells, blood and organs?

Is your movie creating a marinade that is bathing your cells in loving chemicals like dopamine and oxytocin, or is it activating your negative chemicals, adrenaline and cortisol? You are what you think. It's not just what happens to you that creates your experience and life. It is what you do with your experience by way of your thoughts and interpretations that ultimately determine the outcomes!

Your thinking is physical and powerful. It may be worth your while and your life to start paying attention to the movie you are generating inside your mind. Your longevity might benefit from a change in your movie selections.

Another question:

» If you had a bubble rising above your head and your thoughts could be projected into the bubble, what would you see? What would be the monologue or film script that reflects your thoughts?

In the case of the driver cut off on the road, your Victim voice might yell out:

"Why does this have to happen to me?"

"No one really cares that I could have been killed here!"

Or your Survivor voice could kick into action and scream:

"That $%^&#! Who does he think he is? I'll show him he can't get away with this. It's every man for himself!"*

If you are fortunate to have a Navigator voice, you might say:

"Catch your breath. You're getting too worked up. You don't have to give your power away to that jerk. Anyway, he sure

looks like he is in a rush. Maybe there is an emergency he has to take care of."

Take a few deep breaths, try a reframe, remember or re-create a time when you felt safe or connected and then respond.

Think before you speak!

Just because you feel upset, it does not mean you have to take it personally.

These are just a few different ways to think about one incident. Each way will produce a different movie that powerfully determines how you feel and act.

One way of thinking results in feeling like a sad, victimized loser.

A second way of thinking creates an adventure movie, one in which revenge and settling a score are the major themes.

The third way of thinking helps to keep you on track, calm down quickly and be the captain of your own ship, navigating to wherever you want to go.

Your thoughts are like a movie with the sounds and visuals that we project onto our world. We need to remind ourselves that things aren't just happening and start truly appreciating the power of thinking, interpreting and creating personal narratives that we believe are real. As my daughter, Laura, might say, "It's just a movie!"

If your thoughts simply come and go without impacting your body, that would be one thing. But your thoughts are physical. I will repeat that many times in this book. Your thoughts are physical. They powerfully destroy your body, make you sick and even shorten your life.

On the flip side, they also can enliven, enhance and stimulate your cells to create increased health and well-being. In the next chapter, we will take another look at the physical dimension of your thinking.

Key Points

- Life is deceptive because we create our life through our beliefs and interpretations.

- We live out our stories like a movie that we keep replaying and re-experiencing over and over again like in *Groundhog Day*. While we may become addicted to our movies, it is important that we realize we made them up.

- What kind of movie is your life? What title might you name it? Are you enjoying it? Would you go to the movie theatre and pay for a ticket to see it? Who would you choose to play yourself in the movie?

- Your thoughts are physical energies that impact the health and vitality of your body and its emotions.

- In your imagination, what voice most often speaks to you: Navigator, Survivor or Victim? Who has the strongest influence?

- What can you do to increase your Navigator's voice so that you can better hear its call and profit from what it is trying to say to you?

• —— | • | • | • | —— •

Chapter 13:

THE BODY IS A MAP OF THE MIND

Through its sensations, your body expresses a biological manifestation of what you are thinking. In other words, as I stated earlier, your thinking is physical. It manifests physical reactions whether or not you are consciously aware of this fact.

Thoughts are the language of the mind and feelings are the language of the body (Lipton, 1990).

To illustrate, if you spend time thinking about an event about which you are feeling insecure, such as speaking in front of a large group of people, chances are you will, indeed, feel insecure and experience sensations in your body that correspond to these feelings.

Perhaps you will notice tension or butterflies in your stomach. When you picture yourself in front of the group, your heart rate and pulse might jump and your breathing may quicken. Basically, you are conditioning your body with your mind.

According to Bruce Lipton, a neuromedical researcher, the body has a "memorized state" that resists change. If you have been spending some time feeling insecure or worried about something, your body listens carefully to your emotions and develops a memory from that experience.

Your reality is an expression of both your emotions and body memories. This emotional and body memory state can become so powerful that you eventually seek out experiences that conform to your internal state. Since it is the result of your past experience, this state is no more than a lens of the past. It cannot see the "now." Consequently, you may not do a great job of realistically evaluating the situation you are facing. Instead, you are reacting to the emotional state and bodily memory of your past mental movie.

The mind seeks a steady state and no change. Sometimes, like a chick trapped too long inside its shell, you may be stuck in an old way of viewing the world that is too narrow and self-destructive.

If that happens, it might be the right time to peck your way out of misery.

NEURAL PLASTICITY
The good news is that you have a resource that can alter this condition. Your brain has a neural plasticity that allows you to alter the movie that has captured your body

and well-being. Your life does not have to be determined by the emotional state or genetic map from your basic internal roadmap. You can actually alter and change your genetic map.

Your experience, perception and thoughts together have a powerful impact on your map and movie. This is the phenomenon of *epigenesis*, the ability of experience to alter your genetic map or DNA.

To better appreciate the healing power of experience, let's look at how cells work. According to Bruce Lipton, proteins provide for cell structure and function. Life is a function of movement of these proteins.

Movement equates to life; non-movement equates to death.

As Satchel Paige, a baseball pitcher from the 1940s might say, "You have to keep moving to keep the juices flowing."

Yet, these cell proteins do not move on their own. Something has to stimulate or urge the proteins to action. The agent of change is a signal that might be chemical, a toxin, a loud noise or even a thought. The important point here is that the protein requires a signal to move. The actual movement might be a respiratory, digestive, cardiac or muscular one, depending on the protein's location.

EPIGENESIS

Our minds, as expressed through our thoughts, create electrical and chemical energy which signal the cellular protein to move.

Though genes provide the blueprint for our life, as well as the form and structure of our proteins, they do not cause or predict what will happen to us as we age. It is epigenesis, through the signal elicitations of the cell's protein, that creates how your life evolves.

Epigenesis acts through perception. The nervous system perceives something going on around or inside its body, causing a signal to elicit protein movement inside the cell where the genes reside.

Therefore, change your perception; change the reading of your genes.

The bottom line is that perception controls our biology and our lives. Genes do not!

Also, keep in mind that your body houses 100 trillion cells. When you consider that our planet is home to seven billion humans, a pretty vast community, your body is no slight miracle.

Somehow, our immensely crowded internal world works together pretty well. Our legs and arms move us around from place to place throughout the day. Our heart beats more than 100,000 times a day. Our digestive system transforms the food we eat into elements that nurture us. Our elimination system transports waste and toxins outside of our bodies. Our respiratory system provides the oxygen that keeps us alive and thriving.

Somehow the whole community of 100 trillion cells coordinates and functions day after day. You continue to live and, hopefully, thrive.

We make perceptions that trigger protein changes. Our cells figure out how to co-exist with our genes and our bodies persevere.

All is governed by a central force — our mind.

PLACEBOS AND NOCEBOS

Our mind and thoughts are immensely powerful. If you doubt the power of the mind, consider the phenomenon of the placebo and nocebo effects. As you may know, *placebos* are neutral substances which have no scientific medical usefulness. Nevertheless, when they are tested in comparison to active drugs or treatments, they are reported to account for more than one-third of medical cures.

With the *nocebo* effect, people imagine that an inert substance or treatment will be harmful. Based on their perceptions, their imagined worst-case projections come true.

Strong belief in terrible, worst-case scenario predictions can cause cellular proteins to freeze, stopping movement and growth, thus causing illness and possible death.

For example, if your physician, looking soberly at your CAT scan or MRI, reports to you that your medical studies are indicative of a metastatic cancer with no cure, there is a high probability that you will die.

This is true even if he is wrong and has misread your results.

Thinking is physical. In this case, it can dominate your actual physical condition.

GROWTH AND PROTECTION

The purpose of cells is to grow and prosper. Our cells naturally strive toward growth and away from danger.

Stress and the perception of danger go hand in hand. Stress hormones do not promote health; they exist to protect us from harm.

For example, adrenaline and cortisol can shut down the immune system. Blood vessels squeeze and redirect blood to the extremities to prepare for an emergency response such as fleeing or fighting. Blood stops flowing to the viscera. Cellular growth is halted.

In addition, the perception of danger reduces blood flow to the frontal lobes, the seat of thinking and problem solving. Instead, blood flows to the back of your brain, the seat of survival and protection. Instead of thinking clearly, the survival brain instinctively perceives increased risk for danger and decides if it is time to fight or flee.

Stress reactions might save the day but not your life.

The key to a prolonged, healthy life is growth through protein movement. If you truly think you are going to die or your condition is taking a downhill turn, your future can be bleak.

MIND AND BODY
The mind and body are not separate entities. All physical activity is controlled by your thoughts and energy vibrations.

As electrical vibrations, your thoughts can powerfully influence what happens to you. While you may not take much notice of your thinking or how your fears and needs impact your physiology, you might be surprised at how much you are being impacted.

Your mind power, what you perceive and think, influences the experiences you have and even the people in which you come into contact.

Focus on fear and chances are you will perceive danger.

Focus on success and you will begin to see a plethora of opportunities at your feet.

Think about your favorite person with whom you feel safe and connected and your brain responds with a healthy surge of dopamine into your nervous system, providing you with a feel-good emotional experience.

Remember, your mind is a creature of habit, easily directed by past experiences. Unfortunately, our minds do a better job at accessing negative memories than positive ones. We have to be cognizant and careful of the fact that 80 percent of our thoughts are negative. That means if you are drawn to worry and suffering, your mind will feed you a steady diet of stress, upset and disappointment.

Plus, it appears that the natural resting or default mode of the brain is a constant state of alertness and vigilance. The Survival Brain scans our world, searching for signs of potential danger or harm. Consequently, we may experience bursts of tension or worry even though there is no real source of danger present.

Interested in success and happiness? Try changing your mind.

If you want external conditions to change, change your internal conditions — your thoughts and beliefs.

I DON'T DESERVE TO BE HAPPY

I am now working with a female patient who is currently being dominated by her internal movie script of not being good enough. She is terrified of rejection, abandonment and being alone. She fears taking responsibility for her own life.

Her subconscious mind has been well trained to believe she is a "loser" and her destiny in life is to accommodate and serve others, even though her heart is not in it. Her basic belief is that she does not deserve to be happy. Consequently, she perceives constant threats of rejection and disapproval all around her.

Her life strategy is to protect herself by constantly giving in to others in the hopes that they will see how good she is and offer her the love she craves. But, because her basic belief is that she does not deserve love or happiness, she is doomed to replay her sad movie over and over again. Even if people do demonstrate loving behavior, she misconstrues it and doesn't allow it to heal her. On top of the mental anguish that her negative thinking patterns have created, her physical health also is suffering. As her stress hormones have taken control, she has experienced bouts of hyperventilation, an increase in allergies, shortness of breath and muscular pain.

Thoughts are physical! They are not just random bursts of sensations that go nowhere with no consequences. They impact and stick to your body. They create your future.

She is a captive of Death Psychology, one in which her bias toward negativity will probably lead her into chronic inflammation in her respiratory and cardiac systems, which will cause her to go prematurely downhill.

Key Points

- Your body is a map of your mind.

- What your mind thinks, your body feels.

- Whatever you think has a direct impact on your body.

- By changing your beliefs and thinking, you change the well-being of your body.

- Your thoughts and beliefs alter your genetic expression. Your genes account for only 35 percent of what happens to you; while your thoughts and life experiences account for almost 65 percent.

- Stressful thinking shuts down cell growth. Shut it down long enough and disease emerges.

- Your mind and its thoughts act like a magnetic force that attracts experiences in the real world that correspond to your thinking.

- As you think, you become!

Chapter 14:

ANCHORS OF ANXIETY

On a more personal note, to demonstrate the dynamics of how all of this works, I want to share two prior experiences that generated a mental movie that caused me considerable pain for many years.

THE CONCERT

As mentioned earlier, I grew up in Brooklyn with my parents and older brother. When I was eight years old, I remember my mother taking me every Saturday morning to the Henry Street Settlement House to attend piano lessons. In early December of my first year of lessons, I learned a few simple songs. Being very proud of my newly learned skill, I asked my second grade teacher if I could play two songs for the elementary school assembly. She smiled broadly and said that I could. She told me that I could do my mini-recital at the next assembly.

I couldn't wait to get home to practice my two songs. I felt no anxiety, just the eager anticipation of entertaining my friends with my new musical skills.

A week later, the assembly was held. It was a week before Christmas. In my school, sliding wooden walls separated the classes. On occasions such as an assembly, the walls were pushed open, thus creating a large space with all the children sitting at their desks.

That day, I stepped onto the stage and took a deep breath. With a big smile, I announced that I was going to play some Thanksgiving and Christmas carols.

Yet, to my dismay, everyone, including the teachers, burst into loud laughter. I had no idea why they were all laughing at me and felt devastated. I perceived their laughter as ridicule rather than appreciation.

Immediately, I felt a blast of uncomfortable heat throughout my body. I was humiliated. As I sat at the piano and played my two songs, tears fell onto my fingers and the keys. Regardless of how I felt, I played on.

After my recital, which included "Over the River and Through the Woods" and "Jingle Bells," I received loud applause, but it was too late. Their laughter had ripped into my body and I felt shame and rejection.

After my recital, I asked my teacher why everyone had treated me that way when I first announced my two songs. She smiled and reached out to touch my shoulder.

"Moss," she began. "I'm so sorry. We weren't laughing at you. It was how you pronounced the words Thanksgiving and Christmas. You see, the reason you go to the speech therapist here at school is because you are learning to say words correctly. It's just that the way you pronounced these words, it sounded like you were saying 'Wanksgiving' and 'Wistmas' carols. We all loved your music and we didn't mean to laugh at you."

My teacher was very thoughtful, supportive and her touch felt comforting, but the damage was done. I had taken the laughter personally and the emotional wound had already penetrated into my emotional brain where words had little reparative power.

THE SPELLING TEST

Years later in the seventh grade, I experienced another big upset. Each week in English class we would have a spelling test on Friday. One test stands out in appalling detail. We had to learn several words that sounded alike but were very difficult for me to discern: "to, too and two" and "there, they're and their."

For the life of me, I struggled. On the next test I failed, along with five others.

On a repeat test one week later, three of us failed.

One week later, a re-examination. I did not fare very well. I had failed the quiz. Consequently, my teacher, Mrs. Levine, stood above me and, in her booming voice, looking down at me like a predatory dinosaur, she exclaimed, "Well Moss Jackson, why is it that everyone else spelled the words correctly and only you failed to do so?"

Under her glare and the giggles of my fellow students, I grappled with finding an adequate answer. I stammered a grunt or two before I looked up at Mrs. Levine's monstrous physical presence. She reminded me of my closet boogeyman from years past.

Mrs. Levine hovered over me repeating her question. I stared at her intently for what felt like an eternity before I answered. I just wanted her to leave me alone.

So I glared back and exclaimed loudly, "My mother died!"

Gasps were heard around the room. My friend Richard whispered, "I didn't know your mother died!"

Mrs. Levine held her hand over her mouth and left the room while all my friends questioned me about my mother's death. Of course she was not dead, but what I said worked.

A few minutes later the vice principal, Mr. Gordon, accompanied my teacher back into the room. Mrs. Levine looked quite pale. Mr. Gordon, kind man, escorted me out and walked me to the local ice cream store where he bought me an ice cream cone.

I had survived the wrath of Mrs. Levine!

I thought the day was won until a week later.

Mrs. Levine handed out a pop quiz with the same three words I had failed to spell correctly. Before doing so, she announced to the class, "In honor of the resurrection of Mrs. Julia Jackson who miraculously came back to life and appeared at last night's PTA meeting, you will all have another go at 'there,' 'their' and 'they're'."

I have no idea how I did on that test but I remember being left with a similar feeling that I had experienced back in second grade. I felt vulnerable, hurt and ashamed.

I think in both situations I concluded that I wasn't smart or good enough. My thought process seemed to be, "Watch out! Danger is lurking. If I take a risk or make a mistake, others will laugh or make fun of me."

THE CURSE IS LIFTED

Although no one ever knew how I felt or what I was thinking, I carried this burden inside of me for years. It was not until my second year of college that I had a corrective experience. I was in Abnormal Psychology, one of my favorite classes, where the Professor said to me, "I really like your questions and I like having you in my class. I want you to consider majoring in Psychology. I think you have a talent for it."

I felt as if a curse had been lifted by his words. Maybe I wasn't stupid after all. Maybe I was smart and talented. In an instant, new neural pathways were already forming in my brain.

That short exchange between my professor, Dr. Williams, and I sent a surge of well-being throughout my body, an antidote for the self-deprecating mindset I had been harboring for years. There is a healing power that we have with each other.

A nurturing and compassionate relationship can go a long way to heal the anxious, insecure and unpredictable patterns that were constructed so many years ago.

In these healing moments, it is possible to get a glimpse of immortality.

Thoughts are powerful. Thoughts are physical.

In all three situations, I had felt the words settle into my body. In the first two cases, I felt the stress and shame flood all over me like a hot bolt of radiation. With my psychology professor, I felt the shame and self-judgment lift, allowing me to breathe again.

I have found that the old adage "Sticks and stones will break your bones but words will never harm you" is false.

Thoughts provoke energy. Strong physical reactions can hurt, paralyze and hamper development in some senses.

Thoughts can be anchors of anxiety that weigh us down, throwing us into protection mode and shutting down personal growth and health. Thoughts also can heal and create well-being.

The brain is a wonderful organ, capable of shifting our experience and transforming our reality. That is why it is our greatest asset in striving for longevity and the possibility of immortality.

Key Points

- Early experiences and the resulting conclusions we form can last a lifetime.

- Thoughts are powerful and physical. Similar to how a sculptor carves a statue with chisel and hammer, we shape our lives through our thoughts and beliefs.

- Words and thoughts settle into our bodies.

- Thoughts can hamper and impair personal development.

- Negative thoughts weigh us down like anxiety anchors, costing us personal growth and vitality.

- Positive thoughts and beliefs can alter our self-concept and reality.

Chapter 15:

A CHEROKEE LEGEND

One time, a young Cherokee boy got into a fight with another boy over a toy. The boy lost the fight and ran in heated anger to his grandfather. He began venting his fury and wished for revenge.

The grandfather listened for a while, then calmly said:

"My son, each of us has two wolves inside our heart. One is the Wolf of Evil and the other is the Wolf of Love. The Wolf of Evil is anger, envy, jealousy, regret, arrogance, self-pity, guilt, resentment, inferiority, lies, false pride, superiority and ego. The Wolf of Love is joy, peace, caring, hope, serenity, humility, kindness, benevolence, empathy, generosity, compassion and faith."

The child thought about it for a while and then asked the grandfather, "Which wolf wins?"

The old Cherokee simply smiled and replied, "The one that you feed."

The story has many versions but the moral remains the same. We have many, many thoughts that run through our conscious minds every day at a rate of more than 2,000 per day. While we may not be conscious of all of our thoughts, they are laying down neural tracks every minute.

Which ones do you pay attention to?

Do you dwell on the driver who cut you off hours ago?

Or the colleague who has not called you back since you left him a message two days ago? Perhaps it is the person who stood you up for a date and you can't stop thinking they probably are not really attracted to you?

On the other hand, you might tend to linger on more positive thoughts and experiences. You daydream about the talk you gave and how many people seemed to appreciate your contribution. While there were some who did not comment or who appeared disinterested, you take in the positive experience and feel a glow of success.

Perhaps you reflect about a sales presentation that did not result in a sale but you think about what you learned from the experience to help you do a better job the next time. You focus on the learning experience rather than the performance part.

And there might be a customer who did not return your call, so you send a text stating you hope everything is okay and that you're thinking about him and wondering if you can be of any service.

It seems that we have more negative thoughts than positive ones. Remember the Alligator Brain a few chapters back? Its role is to watch out for our survival and to protect us from danger. Since it does not discriminate very well between real and perceived threats, it tends to overreact to all of them. "Better safe than sorry" is its operating motto! So what's a little worry or upset? It really does not care very much how you feel, just that you are safe.

I have a patient, Ken, who is a brilliant artist and musician. At the age of 60, he is coming into his own and being recognized for his compositions and fine singing voice. When he is alone composing and working on his music, Ken feels wonderful. He enjoys improvising and experimenting with different arrangements and rhythms. That is, until he starts to think about performing his work in front of an audience. He has an uncanny ability to remember past times when he made a mistake and felt terrible about himself.

Even though his audiences and fans adore him and love his music, he dwells on the missed notes and begins to fret miserably about his future. Ken bounces back and forth between his memories of past mistakes and his future worries about disapproval. He is left with negative states of energy which then interfere with or block his creativity.

Ken's Wolf of Evil is winning the internal struggle! While the external evidence points to his talent and artistic recognition, he focuses and obsesses about a missed note. While others enjoy and are carried away by his music, he sees only that one mistake.

Unless he can find a way to alter his focus, Ken will not be successful. He will continue struggling to improve his skill to no avail if he does not realize that errors and mistakes are part and parcel of success.

If he continues to focus and dwell on what others may think of him, Ken is likely to develop a hypersensitivity to criticism and even perceive disapproval where none actually exists. He will become a "Falling Star" rather than a "Shining Star."

I am working with another patient, Don, a twelfth-grade student about to graduate. He, too, sees through a dark lens, harboring grudges and resentment far beyond a single upsetting situation. Just recently, for example, he and his father had a slight misunderstanding early one morning. Even though his father realized he was overreacting because of his own fatigue and irritability and apologized for snapping, Don continued to hold tightly onto his hurt and anger well into the day.

At school that morning, he had trouble concentrating as he ruminated about the incident earlier that morning.

When I met with him later that afternoon, he was sullen and withdrawn. With some prompting and encouragement from me, he expressed his anger and hatred toward his father. Even though his father had texted him earlier to again apologize and take responsibility for his outburst, Don remained possessed by his "Wolf of Hatred."

Don's wolf was powerful, causing him to experience an emotional hijack in which he lost all sense of connection and love. He wasted almost an entire day plotting revenge and imagining ways to make his father pay for what had happened. He was failing to hold the two wolves in his heart together. He reported that he often required two or three days to let go of his intense reactions and reconnect with his father.

» How about you? Are you prone to negativity or focused on the positive aspects of your life? Who is winning the battle for your heart, the Wolf of Love or the Wolf of Evil?

Remember, your thoughts have energy and carry a physical force throughout your body. The more negativity and stress you focus on, the greater the likelihood of chronic disappointment, fear and physical distress.

Chronic negative thinking is stressful. Like sandpaper on wood, it wears you down, resulting in reduced capacity to enjoy life and sustain health.

Key Points

- There are two wolves that live in our hearts; the Wolf of Love and the Wolf of Evil.

- Which wolf are you feeding?

- We have many more negative thoughts each day than positive ones.

- What kind of food is your Wolf of Love waiting for from you?

- What keeps you from always feeding your Wolf of Love?

Chapter 16:

BREAKTHROUGH TO HEALTH, VITALITY AND LIFE

HOW WE ARE WIRED

I have focused so far on how we are wired and the impact that chronic stress and negative thinking have on our health, vitality, quality of life and potential for longevity.

In summary, we are wired more for negativity than positivity. People go through life as Navigators, Survivors or Victims. Our old Reptilian, or Survival Brain, functions to keep us safe, not happy.

We have a four-to-one ratio of negative to positive thinking. Our thinking carries an energy charge that affects every cell in our body. Too much chronic worrying and stress shut down the life force, while gratitude, appreciation and joy bathe our cells in dopamine and oxytocin, the hormones of feeling good and loved.

We have two forces within us that battle for our attention; the Wolf of Love and the Wolf of Evil. Whichever one you pay more attention to or "feed" naturally grows more powerful.

The Wolf of Evil has an upper hand, since we tend to be wired more toward worry and negative thinking than love, gratitude and appreciation. Yet, the same old pattern of fear, competition, every man for himself, distrust, a daily diet of taking things personally and marinating in an ecology of reactivity does not have to be our collective destiny.

There is a possibility to escape the Wolf of Evil, the invisible Death Psychology that still remains so powerfully present as we move through the first quarter of the 21st century.

For the Wolf of Love to prevail, we have to bring something special into our lives. We do not have to be trapped in replaying the same old movie over and over again. We can change the reel and create a new movie, one called "Living into Immortality."

This will require an extraordinary breakthrough in consciousness and a complete rewiring of our brains and thoughts through some radical actions.

BREAKTHROUGH THINKING

Breakthrough thinking is a set of strategies and practices that can provide the path toward greater self-confidence, vitality, health, living into radical life extension and living into immortality.

Excessive worrying will not promote internal strength, vitality and an enhanced life force. By staying stuck in negative thinking, you will lose your edge, decrease your competence and eventually suffer physical breakdown.

Breakthrough Thinking is a way to escape the gravitational pull of negativity and stress. There are several key ways to learn Breakthrough Thinking and strategies to create a healthier internal world in which you and your cells can thrive. You can learn how to be a Navigator rather than a Survivor or Victim.

Wouldn't you like to escape the world of reactivity and eventual physical inflammation and disease called our Death Psychology and launch yourself into the world of health and even radical life extension?

FOUR KEY QUESTIONS

Let's start with a set of several breakthrough questions into immortal thinking you can ask yourself. These questions are often thought about by Life Navigators and people who are engaged in creating extraordinary lives of success, accomplishment and satisfaction. The four questions are:

1. Do you have a compelling vision?

2. What is the purpose that drives you?

3. Who is the person you have to be to feel like you have reached success?

4. How do you have to rewire your brain to live an extraordinary life?

1. Do you have a compelling vision to wake up to?

A vision is a compelling picture of your future, an idealized state that energizes your actions toward success. It spells out your future direction and where you see yourself headed. For example, Martin Luther King's vision, "I have a dream" served to guide him and millions of people toward racial equality and dignity. Steve Jobs' vision was to create Internet gadgets that dazzled the imagination. Mark Zuckerberg came up with the world's hottest social networking site, Facebook. President Kennedy had a vision to land a man on the moon and safely bring him back, even though there was no known technology present to make that happen.

Companies often have vision statements too. Nike brings inspiration and innovation to every athlete in the world. Toys "R" Us' motto is to put joy in kids' hearts and a smile on parents' faces. Amazon aims to be the earth's most customer-centric company, to build a place where people can come to find anything they might want to buy online.

Personal vision statements can be powerful energizers and change over time as people move into different life stages. When I was in high school, my goal was to break a 38-year half-mile track record. In college, it was to not get kicked out and to earn my B.A.

As a young psychologist, it was to be the most sought-after practitioner in my area. One of my visions now is to write a best-selling book.

Another is to live an extraordinary life at least until age 125, at which time I can decide what to envision next!

Your vision statement gives your life a direction, a target to move toward. It is your North Star, a beacon that keeps you on track even when you are pulled in different directions. It is great to have a dream, something that you desire or crave. What makes a vision different from a dream is that a vision is a dream with a plan. You need a map to move from where you are now toward the desired state.

In this regard, I think of the character Indiana Jones. He always seemed to be working toward some challenge or some ancient acquisition but kept getting buffeted by one obstacle after another. Thank God for his precious map that he kept using to remind him where he was and the next step he had to take to continue toward his destination. For him, no map meant no success.

For you and me, without a plan, our vision becomes an elusive dream.

David Kekich is a pioneer and Navigator in the field of radical life extension who has devoted his professional life to finding a cure for aging, not exactly a small vision. I asked his permission to reprint here a recent correspondence where he described his vision.

"Imagine never again being able to reflect on your past and never being able to plan for your future. What a horrible prospect, don't you think? Isn't it worth a little effort to extend life's pleasures and accomplishments for as many years as possible? Well, in 1998, I made myself a promise. Not only did I resolve to extend your life and mine, but I determined we would never have to die, at least not from aging.

A year later, I incorporated Maximum Life Foundation. Its purpose was to reverse — yes, reverse — the human aging process. That means not only would we stop biological aging, but we have targeted full rejuvenation for the elderly, essentially resetting your aging clock to when you were in your prime.

Currently, 100,000 people die every day from aging. And nearly all linger and suffer horribly from the diseases and conditions that lead to aging-related death. We're going to stop that. Period. And we're determined to do it by 2033, thus preserving the world's ultimate resources: its 7 billion human minds."

James Strole and Bernadeane, the directors of People Unlimited, inspired me to write this book. This is their vision:

> "For over 50 years, we've carried a vision in our bodies of a world without sickness, aging and death. A world where people can get exponentially better and stronger with a true sense of joy. We know there will never will be an end to human beings' tendency to destroy themselves and others until death is eradicated. The death urge is deeply embedded in the genetics and inflicts constant chaos in the body. We must be as alive as we can be to root out old patterns and ideas that inhibit us, so that we might realize our true endless potential, and embrace and support everything along the way that can enhance our staying alive. Together we will create a humanity that's dedicated to biological immortality rather than mortality, so that all are energy can go into building a continuously new and better human existence."

Here is the vision of **Dr. Bill Andrews**, a leading radical life extension scientist in the field of telomeres.

"Immortality is a lot more complex than just curing aging. Curing aging doesn't prevent us from being run over by busses or falling off cliffs; we can still be killed. Curing aging may decrease our risks of cancer and heart disease but it won't completely eliminate them. To be immortal we need to solve these latter things also. Fortunately, there are scientists working to find ways to freeze our bodies (called cryonics) and thaw them later when cures for cancer, heart disease, and other death causing illness become available. And, there are other scientists working on mind uploading (also called Whole Brain Emulation) so that simultaneously with our airbags opening up during fatal accidents our minds are uploaded to a computer that can later download our minds to other bodies. These things combined with organ replacement and artificial body parts could feasibly make us immortal. The only question that would remain is "are we still we?" But, then again, I would rather be a mind in another body downloaded from a computer, or frozen for thousands of years, or be completely replaced with cultured or robotic body parts, than be a decaying brain in the ground or in a heap of ashes.

I can't begin to guess how long people living today will live but I wouldn't be surprised that many of us live to be 250-500 years. And, the longer we live the more likely we can become immortal."

2. What is the purpose that drives you?

If vision is where you want to go, your purpose is the reason for doing it and why your quest is important. Here are some examples:

Victor Frankel was a Jewish neurologist in Austria who, along with his wife and children, was captured and thrown into German concentration camps during WWII. For several years he was tortured, starved and exhausted. Somehow, even throughout the misery, each day he noticed something to appreciate and value.

To him, living a life of purpose saved his life. He created a belief that if a person knows the "why" or purpose of his life, he can tolerate the "what" of his life, all the things that come your way.

For example, on a particularly brutal day, walking back from a heavy day of labor and trudging through the snow, he was known to pause, look at the setting sun, and say something like, "Look at that sunset! Have you ever seen anything more beautiful?" His purpose was to find meaning to live a life of gratitude and appreciation.

Frankel not only saw the sunset: he caught a glimpse into the eternal mind, the world of living an immortal life. In that search, he attained a state of psychological immortality.

There are many examples of people glimpsing into the immortal life of their goals.

There is a website called Portrait of an Angel that is dedicated to helping those move on who feel guilt and suffering from the death of a favorite pet. Its mission is, "I'm a one-woman campaign to stomp out guilt, the kind of guilt that clings like a leech to the coattails of our grief."

In another example, **Soraya** is a Latin pop singer whose mission is to educate women about breast cancer. She hopes to inspire women to take control of their own breast health.

Char, a Spiritual-Intuitive and medium, states that her mission is to remove the fear of death by proving that we don't die and will see our loved ones again. She also wants to remove the fear of living, by showing how we can tap into our wisest selves and make our lives much easier and happier.

Ronnie Oldman, a data-integration solutions sales person, aims to find happiness, fulfillment and value in living.

Like these positive individuals, I also have a purpose. My mission statement is to live a radically extended and extraordinary life, one of success, accomplishment and satisfaction; one transformed through the possibility of immortality, the end of our inherited Death Psychology.

3. Who is the person you have to be to succeed?

Just because you have vision and a purpose to live does not necessarily lead to success and a great life. A key ingredient to living an extraordinary and successful life is to take on the qualities, skills and attitudes of someone who is capable of accomplishing the goals you have defined for yourself. Who you are currently might not be quite up to the task that you have ordained for yourself.

Dick Vermeil, one of the most successful NFL coaches in football history, once shared with me an interesting observation about coaching. Dick was voted Coach of the Year at the high school, college and professional levels. He shared the statistics about what it took to succeed. Only a small percentage of high school players qualified to play college football. An even smaller percentage of varsity college players, around one percent, made it to the pro level.

Each advance required a whole new level of excellence. Excellence at one level did not necessarily predict success at the next level. Each time, both the players and himself as a coach had to reinvent themselves in order to advance.

In another example, **Rich,** a friend of mine, and I were talking recently about success. He had recently gone out on a limb to significantly expand his business. Having taken on a fair amount of debt, he realized that the safety and security of his 200-employee company now depended on his ability to achieve his vision. He remarked to me that it is one thing to earn $25,000. But, to move into the $100,000 range, other skills and qualities would be necessary. And to be the owner and president of a multi-million-dollar national company competing with first-tier champions, he would have to take on the persona of someone much bigger than he now was. He would have to learn the intricacies of running a national rather than a local business. This would require him to think more strategically rather than tactically, learn to negotiate bigger projects and become more confident now that he was playing with the "big boys."

He was experiencing an existential crisis of identity. If he changed, would he stop being the person he was? The answer is yes!

He stepped into this new identity with anxiety and excitement. Fortunately, his vision and purpose were powerful enough to pull him forward into action, learning to manage his anxiety through each step. Without a clear vision, purpose and personal redesign of his identity, his anxiety would have won the day and he would have either failed to reach his goals or died in the process.

4. Rewiring your brain

If you made it this far in terms of articulating your vision, clarifying your purpose and reconstituting your identity, there remains the task of rewiring your brain. It is one thing to drive a commercially sold car through city traffic and another thing to handle a sophisticated race car capable of speeding around a track at 200 miles an hour. New skills, timing, eye-hand coordination, exceptional peripheral vision and split-second decision making are required to survive, much less win.

Likewise, as you strive to succeed outside your comfort zone, you will have to rewire your brain.

For example, I have a vision to write a bestseller and my purpose is to live an extraordinary life of success, accomplishment and satisfaction. Underlying this desire, I have a compelling internal drive to create. I move through my days looking for any way possible to create. Whether in my role as therapist, success coach, writer or life navigator, it seems the more I generate from my inventive side, the more my hunger for creativity grows.

As I rewire my brain to become more open, flexible and divergent, I see more and more opportunities to experiment and create.

As I rewire the neural networks for creativity in my brain, I seem to see and attract more opportunities to create, and break free from my own Death Psychology. To live a radically long and healthy life, I am replenishing my toolbox with new life-enhancing beliefs, meditation and mindfulness practices, along with genetic studies and re-designed eating and exercise programs.

MINDFULNESS PRACTICES
For example, every morning on my drive to work, I conduct a mindfulness practice. I ask myself the following three questions:

» What do I want to experience?

» What do I want to learn?

» What do I want to contribute?

The answers to these questions become my roadmap for the day. I think the answers become absorbed into my subconscious; seldom do I pause during the day to consider how I am doing. Yet, I notice the day seems to fly by. I enjoy myself a lot more and finish the day feeling refreshed and energized.

These questions are different from how I used to approach the day. I used to think differently. I would think about how many patients I was seeing, what responsibilities and tasks I needed to handle and what problems or crises might show up.

I think my three new questions are helping me to daily rewire my brain, thus giving me a whole new reality. At times, I can almost feel the physical rewiring in my brain! It feels like I let a construction crew renovate my internal home while I go about the business of the day.

I have also had my nutritional genotype analyzed. The genotype is a survival strategy that our ancestors worked out over the past 100,000 years. It is the result of interactions between genetic heritage, pre-natal experiences and our daily relationship with the environment, including diet and exercise. These elements tend to fall into predictable patterns, usually one of six basic genotype diets. My own pattern falls into the Hunter profile. The profile also comes with a list of foods that complement my Nutritional genotype, and a list of those foods to avoid.

I also am participating in a Male Blood Panel through *Life Extension Magazine* for a thorough study of my metabolic system. This should provide me with a deeper understanding of my physiology so that I can better select supplements, vitamins and herbs that will benefit me for continued health, balance and vitality.

I also have completed the "23 and Me" analysis to better grasp my future well-being so that I can better navigate my medical progress and not wait until my physician diagnoses me with an illness that could have been prevented years before.

These tools and actions will help me better understand and manage my health, metabolic and nutritional needs. As I continue to learn about my genetic foundations with regard to possible organ vulnerabilities and potential disease, I can better take preventive actions to enhance my physical stamina and resistance.

"Forewarned is fore-armed" is a useful expression that Navigators use to help them make decisions and choose action paths that promote successful and healthy living. These tools and practices are expressions of an immortal lifestyle. As you can see, I am doing my utmost to fly faster than illness and the speed of death!

Illness is often a result of many small choices we inadvertently make over the years. "Knowledge is power!" If we can better predict what lies ahead, we can choose to do something different and alter our course of action.

So, what are you out to accomplish? Chances are, if you are working outside your comfort zone and shooting for something extraordinary, you will have to do some rewiring, too.

If you are up for something big such as a change in career or creating a personal vision that will take you out of your comfort zone, much less living into immortality, then take the time to review your vision, purpose, and actions required for success and well-being.

Success, well-being and life extension go hand in hand. You could attain considerable success like many Survivor types do but pay the price of chronic stress, anxiety, anger, inflammation and disease.

I strongly suggest you take the time to think about what you are envisioning and plan accordingly to keep yourself healthy and vital.

After all, what's the point of attaining success if you are sick or dead?

Key Points

- We are more wired for negativity than for positive thinking.

- People go through life as Navigators, Survivors or Victims.

- Our Survivor Brain is not interested in our happiness, just our safety.

- Breakthrough thinking offers us a map and strategy into vitality and health.

- Breakthrough thinking answers four basic questions.

  1. What is my vision?
  2. What is my purpose?
  3. Who do I have to be to succeed?
  4. What actions must I take to rewire my brain?

· —— | · | · | · | —— ·

Chapter 17:

BREAKTHROUGH THINKING

Answers to the four key questions in the previous chapter give you a structure for success: a **direction**, **purpose**, **identity** and a **design** to rewire your brain and give yourself a fighting chance to emerge from any rut. This strategy also gives you something big to shoot for, a vision much larger than your current capacity to thrive.

To achieve an extraordinary level of satisfaction, life-extension and well-being requires a different kind of thinking, being and doing. Your old and familiar life formula probably does not have the propulsion power to free you from the gravitational pull of negativity and worry. If you have articulated a new life perspective, it would be helpful to have some tools to launch you into a different orbit in which to explore and navigate.

WHAT IS BREAKTHROUGH THINKING?
The Breakthrough Thinking Model described by Dudley Lynch in his groundbreaking book, *Strategy of The Dolphin* (1989) offers an excellent structure for redesigning and retooling your formula for success, your identity and your future.

In general, it seems that most people avoid and actively resist change. Perhaps the key to appreciating this notion is to ask, "How bad do things have to get before someone changes?"

Brenda

Brenda, a 40-year-old patient, has been miserable in her marriage for the past 20 years. Her relationship with her mother is contentious and she feels unappreciated at work. No matter how hard she tries, no one seems satisfied or appreciative of her efforts.

By nature, she is an accommodator who hopes to win approval and acceptance by going overboard to give others what they want.

People in her life often take advantage of her good nature, causing her to feel increasingly resentful and hurt. She is depressed, angry and recently suffered respiratory and muscular weakness. Her immunological resistance is getting weaker and she is a candidate for experiencing further physical and emotional breakdown.

She feels she does not deserve to be happy if it means asserting herself and setting boundaries with others.

Her operating motto is "If others really cared, they would show it."

The question here is how far down into disintegration does Brenda have to go before she gets the courage to stand up for herself?

Brenda is what we call a late adopter, a very late adopter, and maybe she just waited too long. Things might have to become drastic and life-threatening before she is willing to break out of her life-depleting patterns and join a life of vitality and vision. Then again, she may choose to remain stuck and trapped in her limited world view, continue to suffer and slide downward into a state of permanent unhappiness and powerlessness. In a fashion, she has the power to pronounce a death sentence on herself.

Nick

Nick is another case. He is a successful, good-looking and healthy salesman who is happily married. Recently, upon turning 60 years old, he realized that his entire adult life had been focused on work. He is now aware of a desire for friendships and social activities. Having come from a blue collar family that struggled with financial issues, he has good insight into the work dynamic. He promised himself to never be poor and has succeeded in that vision.

He is now looking at a new vision and a strategy to move in that direction. Unlike Brenda, Nick is taking action much earlier in the change process. He is not at risk for emotional stress or physical breakdown. Nick is an Early Adapter. He is creating a life worth living.

Steve Jobs

Steve Jobs was brilliant in his role at Apple Computer in creating change before there was a need for change or a crisis that demanded a reaction. He thrived on stirring things up at work, often announcing a development and later launch of a new or improved product line. While others around him may have felt distressed about not knowing exactly what to do or what problems might get in the way, Jobs was enthralled by his imagination and creative brilliance. He was an innovator such that others had to catch up and adapt to the changes he initiated.

Dolphins and Surfers

Dudley Lynch was fascinated by change and Breakthrough Thinking. He was intrigued by people who were steeped in the change process and curious about others who seemed to wait until life pushed them into taking charge and making a change. He suggested that success and living a great life were a function of timing. His analogy came from watching dolphins and humans surfing waves.

Dolphins and master surfers catch the wave at the most useful time, right when the wave is beginning to curl. If the surfer jumps the gun and starts too early, there is no power to propel him into a great ride. He just has to flounder awhile, bide his time and prepare for the next wave.

On the other hand, if he waits too long, the wave will crash over him and knock him off of his surfboard. After the wipe out, he needs time to recover his breath, reorient himself and decide if he is up for the next wave.

THE KEY TO LIFE NAVIGATION

A key to living a great life is to initiate the change when there are early signs of difficulty or stagnation. Too soon an action and you might not have taken full advantage of your situation. Wait too long after many signs of distress and frustration, and you may not have the power or positioning to launch into another initiative. In fact, the longer you wait, the more power you lose. You will pay the price from delay, avoidance and procrastination. Your life will then pass you by, costing you wasted time and energy. At this point, life becomes more of a cost than an investment. Yet sometimes the cost means you lose your life.

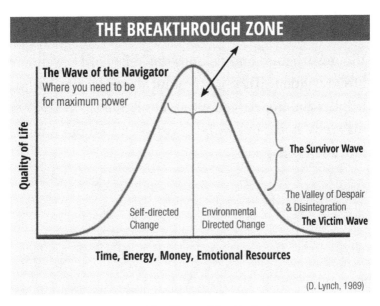

THE BREAKTHROUGH ZONE

The Wave of the Navigator
Where you need to be
for maximum power

Quality of Life

The Survivor Wave

The Valley of Despair
& Disintegration
The Victim Wave

Self-directed
Change

Environmental
Directed Change

Time, Energy, Money, Emotional Resources

(D. Lynch, 1989)

GRAPH #1: The Wave of the Navigator

Life Navigators catch the wave of change early on. They are willing to take a chance and let go of the past. They convert their dreams into visions which, in turn, draw them into radical actions for change. They tend to be inner or self-directed, relying on a combination of logical insights, intuitions and courage to do something different. Their desire to travel in the direction of their vision is stronger than their fear of failure or social disapproval.

Survivors and Victims wait too long before taking action and tend to be pushed by externally driven forces. Survivors take action usually with a strong degree of frustration, resentment and anger. Though they eventually do take action, they bring with them a residue of excessive negative energy.

Victims languish and fall into the Valley of Despair and Disintegration. They get ground down by life, feeling helpless and hopeless about never catching a break. They may have hope, but without vision and action, nothing much really happens.

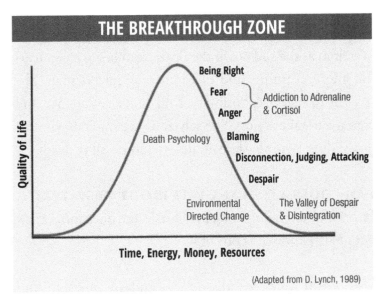

GRAPH #2: The Cost of Waiting Too Long

If you are out to live an extraordinary long life of success, accomplishment and satisfaction, it pays to live like a dolphin, a skilled surfer or a Life Navigator. Know where you are going, why you are going there. Upgrade your persona to match the challenge. Then, rewire your brain by learning the new skills, beliefs and attitudes to move you through the change.

Take action early on with or without any guarantee of success. You learn along the way.

A DEATH PSYCHOLOGY

If you choose to stay stuck, wait too long and suffer, you will then let the environment take control. This is living a Life of Reactivity, what I call a Death Psychology (Refer to the above graph #2). This is the world Brenda found herself in as she slid down the slope from being right, fearful, angry, blaming, and disconnecting into despair. She refused to take responsibility, find inner confidence and courage to take action. She stayed in her miserable box of life, sliding fast into despair, illness and possibly death.

HOW DOES A FISH KNOW IT IS OUT OF WATER?
In *Breakthrough Thinking*, Lynch asks the question, "How does a fish know it is out of water?"

Fish out of water feel discomfort and are quick to find another pool of water. Life Navigators sometimes find themselves like a fish out of water. They experience the discomfort and begin to slide onto the downward slope of living. Yet, they do not stay there very long. When quality of life diminishes, they do not go along with the related life situations.

Life often throws people a curve ball or difficult times. It could be a lost relationship, a failed business or an illness. Pain occurs, but if you languish too long feeling sorry for yourself or blame the world, you are in danger of prolonged and deep suffering.

Navigators detest suffering. Pain may be necessary and tolerable but not the prolonged misery of suffering. Pain comes from not getting what you want. Suffering is what you add to your pain in terms of blame or guilt rather than learning from your situation and getting back on track.

Life Navigators are alert, quick to respond to any sense of life destiny that causes aches and suffering. They are resilient and reorient themselves by asking themselves the four key questions: Where am I going? Why am I going there? Who do I have to be to get there? And how do I have to rewire my brain? They do not accept for very long the feeling of being a fish out of water. Instead, they quickly find a new pool of water to navigate toward.

LIFE IS AN INVESTMENT

Life Navigators become used to the feeling of being eager to re-engage. They harness their focus back toward their visions and identify what tools they need to launch and travel into their breakthrough zones. They are Life Investors, always open to enhancing their well-being, health and vitality.

Too busy living and navigating life, they do not wait until they are in the death spiral spinning out of control toward personal despair and disintegration. They do not just survive life; they live life. This is the essence of psychological immortality.

Psychological immortality involves living into your personal vision and discovering how to do it along the way.

Love your life. Invest in it fully. Put all of your eggs in one basket.

Declare your direction. Be clear about your life purpose, then begin redesigning yourself to be the person who can reach your vision.

Now you have a powerful chance to live a life you will love, one that challenges you to use your fully-integrated brain to create an ongoing sense of safety, connection and personal power. The easy part is pulling the tools you will need to deliver the result.

Key Points

- Most people resist change.

- Change is uncomfortable.

- Survivors often wait until things get really bad before they take action and change.

- Navigators are constantly open to change and are looking for opportunities to take a risk and take action.

- While Navigators sometimes also can wait too long before acting, they learn from the experience and take action sooner the next time.

- Navigators invest their energy, thinking and other resources in Breakthrough Thinking and moving toward their visions. For them, life is an investment, not a cost.

- Navigators quickly learn the signals of falling into the downward slope of disintegration and move to invent more nourishing ways to meet their challenges.

- Psychological immortality centers on surrendering to your vision and launching into your Breakthrough Zone. In the process, your physical vitality, energy and health are enhanced.

- In Breakthrough Living, you are fully engaging your mind and brain to promote an experience of "thriving, not just surviving."

• —— |•|•|•| —— •

Chapter 18:

THE REWIRING OF THE BRAIN

What is your "next body of water?" Do you have a vision, something that has a powerful pull?

Your vision is something you construct out of nothing. You make it up. It requires no proof, material substance, social validation or clear path. It is a deeply held dream, a desire or quest you feel you must pursue. You can often feel it in your body, like an unquenchable thirst. It can consist of becoming an author, a dog rescuer, an inventor, performing on stage or leading a company to be best-in-class, or if you are up for the challenge, even living into a life of psychological and physical immortality.

THE FOUR-MINUTE MILE

Roger Bannister, a British medical student, had a vision that he would become the first runner to break the four-minute mile. The accepted medical belief at the time in the early 1950s was that the human body did not have the capacity to tolerate the physiological stress that running at such a pace and distance required. The heart system was thought to be incapable of weathering the pounding it would have to endure. It would simply give out.

Runners had tried for hundreds of years to break the four-minute mark to no avail. In some instances, runners even had bulls running right behind them to increase their incentives. No matter what, the fastest time set in the 1940s was 4:01 and the record had stood for a decade.

THE BREAKTHROUGH MOMENT

Bannister was expected to win the 1,500-meter Olympic race held in Helsinki in 1952. He came in fourth place and was devastated by his performance. For months, he considered never competing again; his shame and humiliation had shaken him to the core. But, his medical training gave him a strategy.

As a medical student, Bannister researched oxygen consumption. He discovered that consistently paced laps consumed less oxygen than laps of variable speeds. He was forming the GPS in his brain that would eventually become his map to break the mile record.

He also had a vision that he imagined every day. He worked to bypass the critical parts of his mind by creating an absolute certainty than he would break the record. He visualized himself running the race over and over again. In his own imagery, he was making the un-doable do-able.

THE RACE

When the starter fired his gun on the breezy evening of May 6, 1954, Bannister sprinted into the lead. As he ran, he later described it as if his "legs seemed to meet no re-sistance at all, as if propelled by some unknown force." He finished the race a trace under four minutes. By ⁹⁄₁₀ths of a second, he earned his redemption and place in ath-letic history. He also re-calibrated all expectations of what the human body was capable of achieving.

The four-minute mile had been previously described as a brick wall by an American runner named Landy. For Bannister, the brick wall was a frame of reference that needed to be reframed.

He broke through the biggest wall of all, the mind.

The moral of this feat is that when you become certain of something, when every part of you believes it and you surrender to your vision, you rewire your brain. Because you focus on it over and over again, something "magical" can happen. Your brain then focuses on what you are visioning and deletes everything else.

Some refer to this as the Law of Attraction or an intensi-fication of the Reticular Activating System (RAS). The Reticular Activating System is the portion of the brain that focuses your attention and allows for sustained con-centration. As a result, you cease to pay attention to all the stories and negativity that could easily throw you off your path and into doubt.

Every day you are bombarded by thousands of unconscious thoughts and self-talk, 80 percent of which are negative. Fortunately, our subconscious, that automatic, habitual part of the brain, takes on most of this challenge, along with keeping our bodies running reasonably smoothly. It keeps us breathing, our blood cells flowing and nourishing our organs, our digestive system processing the foods we eat, our internal temperature staying in the 98-degree range and other life-sustaining functions. It keeps us balanced and able to walk from one place to another or to drive a car and talk at the same time. It is a remarkable part of our nervous system that works 24/7 out of our awareness and, without it, we would all probably get overwhelmed, confused and go quite mad.

Our conscious mind functions to help us focus, vision, solve problems, plan and organize. Sometimes our conscious thoughts trigger our daydreaming and memories and we find ourselves back in the world of the subconscious, jostled back and forth between those thousands of negative thoughts. It also manages about 2,500 conscious thoughts a day, with 2,000 as negative such as worrying, stewing over something or languishing in past regrets.

Still, it is a remarkable system that allows us to keep our relationships and connections intact, stay focused and on course to live a life of purpose and accomplishment.

Neither system — conscious or subconscious — if it remains stuck in only coping and regulating all these thousands of thoughts, will make you happy or lead to an extraordinary life.

They function to make sure we survive and cope from one day to the next.

For something extraordinary, we need a way of thinking which pulls us into a more focused and less distracted thought, emotional and action strategy.

Become absorbed in something you love. When you both become absorbed and work it through, you will experience an immensely satisfying life.

The process, regardless of the outcome, becomes a rewarding experience. It requires an ability to create something and to surrender your conscious and subconscious minds to the experience. Life Navigators break into this energy. They are in what is called a state of flow.

Breakthrough thinking is a strategy to help you to launch yourself toward your vision. Launch into a state of flow, know where you going, why you are going there and who you have to be to make it happen. You will also need some skills to get you there.

DISCOVERY

A crucial skill is Discovery, learning from your experiences, getting rid of what does not work and keeping those things that lead you in the direction of your vision. If you have created something important or even extraordinary to achieve, you probably will not have a proven or workable formula to achieve your goals. You have to learn along the way, experiencing many mistakes and failures as you proceed. This is especially true in the early stages of your pursuit when you may have few resources or a clear map of steps to take. Chances are, though, if you hang in this Discovery stage long enough, you will, like Roger Bannister, find a path to follow.

In Discovery, there is a lot of experimentation and learning along the way. Mistakes are frequent. They can be frustrating and even discouraging. By being open to mistakes and developing a learning perspective, you move through mistakes, making improvements each step of the way. Not only do you learn what works, but you also develop a powerful mindset and rewire your brain to be resilient, to bounce back and to continue persevering toward your ultimate goal.

RESILIENCE

Another tool is Resilience, an ability to keep bouncing back from failure and disappointments and trying again.

I have a new client, a second-year college student, Patrick, who wants to get good grades, have a girlfriend, entertain a thriving social life and play in a band. He also happens to be a perfectionist who demands that he excel in everything. He keeps running into his "brick wall" of failure, never living up to his expectations.

Self-loathing, frustration and obsessive negative self-talk follow, leaving him wasting time and lamenting his bleak future. In this state, he only feels worse.

He is a master of reactivating his subconscious mind and its never-ending museum tour of past regrets and perceived failures. His negative thinking and self-talk then jettison him into concluding that his life will never change and his future will just reflect his past failures. Now in therapy, he is learning how to self-regulate, visualizing a more successful and balanced life and taking actions that provide some source of satisfaction.

Each time his expectations are not fulfilled, he is now able to bounce back after each disappointment. He also reminds me of the Greek legend Sisyphus, a tragic figure doomed to roll a large boulder again and again up a long hill, never to succeed and each day repeating his ordeal.

Patrick, determined to find satisfaction, knows he is trapped in his perfectionistic fantasies, but keeps trying to succeed. He does not give up. He is learning how to learn and lower his expectations. He is, in essence, learning to be resilient.

There are three other skills which concern the wiring of your brain. We will explore these in a later chapter. But first we need to understand the power of early experience, decision making and beliefs. To accomplish this, we need to revisit the internal world of our emotional, logical and survival brains.

Key Points

- We make our visions up.

- Visions reflect our dreams and passions.

- Visions create certainty in our world of confusion, negativity and reactivity.

- A vision is your GPS in life — a compass reading of your True North.

- Breakthrough thinking gives you a strategy to launch yourself into the world where your vision lives.

- There are a number of useful tools you can use for Breakthrough Thinking, two of which are Discovery and Resilience.

Chapter 19:

YOUR EMOTIONAL BRAIN AND ITS APPETITES

Gorillas eat a lot of bananas. Although not the most intelligent species on the planet, they know something about pleasure, pain and relationships.

Gorillas want to feel good. That's why they gorge on bananas, throw coconuts at hungry lions and swing on vines the entire day.

They do not tolerate pain. Maybe that is why they pound on their chests and make a lot of noise. If they have to fight, they prefer to avoid and minimize pain. Consequently, fights do not last long: a lot of ranting, chest expansion and running back and forth making threatening gestures.

And, when it comes to relationships, they seek to bond with their peers and engage in taking care of each other. They spend a lot of time grooming each other. Gorillas are social animals, very different from their Alligator and Computer neighbors.

THE EMOTIONAL BRAIN
The emotional brain is our Gorilla ancestor. At the emotional level, our primate brain has an appetite for pleasure and seeks those we love and trust. It is our kinship brain, desiring unconditional loyalty, connection and love. This need to bond and nurture distinguishes mammals from other types of animals.

All mammals, be they gorillas, monkeys, porpoises, whales or humans, share the desire and urge to bond and connect.

Bonding studies on infants and young children indicate some interesting observations. During WWII, Rene Spitz studied infants separated from their parents and placed in orphanages. Infants who were simply fed and had their diapers changed but not given much nurturing attention fared badly. Sadly, almost 30 percent suffered emotional and intellectual deficits. Many became ill, depressed and died. While their physiological needs were adequately tended to, it was the lack of physical touch, eye contact and affectionate behaviors from their caretakers that appeared to be at the root of their difficulties.

Other infants who received both physical and emotional care thrived and displayed normal development.

Animal studies show similar findings. At the University of Wisconsin, Harry Harlow and other researchers explored the impact of emotional attachment and separation on infant monkeys. Monkeys who were only fed with no other types of care or connection failed to thrive and many were permanently impaired. Later on, they experienced difficulty bonding with their peers and caring for their own offspring after giving birth.

On the other hand, monkeys who were played with, talked to and given affection such as being held or stroked, grew up without apparent difficulty and were able to both bond with their peers and raise their young.

Children who are raised in a home of secure attachments where there is a reliable presence of care, safety and connection to others tend to thrive much more successfully than children raised in a relationship characterized by inconsistency, unreliable care, lack of safety or broken connection.

Our early social experiences seem to carry enormous weight in defining the quality and satisfaction of our later relationships. Early on, it is not only our physical bodies that need caring, but our emotional brains as well.

POWER OF CONNECTION

For mammals to thrive, connection seems to be essential. Bonding behavior, play and nurturing all contribute to the brain's normal development and the capacity to connect and interact. Humans, in particular, need to form kinships and close communities. This usually occurs in their families, but other types of connections with siblings, peers, mentors and groups all can offer ameliorative and corrective experiences if children fail to receive nurturing behaviors from their families. Without such closely-held relationships, children and adolescents fail to thrive or learn how to connect with others.

The Gorilla or Emotional Brain hungers for connection and nurturing behaviors from others. Without such input, individuals are in danger of developmental delays, intellectual and learning difficulties and social malfunctioning.

Henry
Henry, an adult patient who I have been working with for several years, suffered severe neglect as a child. His father was a cold, distant and abusive man who had little regard for his children. A successful businessman, he valued his acquisitions and wealth but not his family. Henry's mother was a withdrawn and depressed woman who had little energy or interest in caring for the children. She was just too beaten down to nurture. She, too, needed loving behaviors but, because of the marital dysfunction, had trouble connecting to her children or creating a mutually loving relationship with them. Everyone was basically left to survive on their own.

Henry learned to survive, growing up to become extremely successful and rich. Unfortunately, he could not form close relationships with his peers, women or his own family. His hatred for his father was intense and they broke off all contact when Henry was a teen. Henry grew up to fend for himself, mistrusting others and "getting the other guy" before he was taken advantage of. He was lonely, resentful and mistrustful.

While married, he and his wife had a mutually antagonistic relationship where both physical and verbal assaults were common. In addition, he was suffering from high blood pressure, abnormal chronic secretions of adrenaline and cortisol, anxiety, unregulated rage and loneliness.

Anxiety had reached such a high level that he was told by his physician that he would have a heart attack, stroke or some inflammatory disease within the year if he continued with his current lifestyle. He was self-medicating with alcohol, drugs and indiscriminate sex. At the age of 44, his doctor was giving him a death sentence by the time he reached 50 years old.

After an initially tense series of sessions, Henry formed a connection with me as his therapist. Confronting him directly, acknowledging his emotional pain and the sadness underlying his belligerent and angry demeanor, I was able to break through his wall and form a caring and nurturing relationship with him. He slowly grew to recognize his limiting beliefs and behaviors and to take responsibility to change. New neural pathways were developing for a revitalized connection to others.

He now desires more love in his life and the need to radically change who he has been so that others can feel safe with him. He now sees how he has pushed people away from him over the years, including his wife, children and colleagues, in order to protect himself from further rejection and abandonment. Henry identified his underlying belief that he was unlovable and is now developing more self-caring beliefs.

He has worked to limit his alcohol intake and no longer creates such marital havoc where sexual acting out is necessary for him to feel loved and valued. While he slips back into self-defeating bouts of anger, emotional cutoffs and retaliation, he does so less frequently and is able to use the wave of early change to alter his downward spiral. Each time, he rewires his brain to recognize his mistake and to get back on a more productive path.

Henry is learning how to be a Life Navigator, where his Wolf of Love has a better chance of thriving and expressing itself, and creating a life worth living into.

FEEDING THE GORILLA WITHIN US

Your emotional brain needs to be fed, not with bananas but with self-care and bonding behaviors. For some of us, it is hard to give ourselves permission to feel lovable and worthy of nurturing relationships. If you want to increase the power of feeling cared for and caring for others, here are some actions you can take.

SHARING AND GENEROSITY

- Stop being stingy. Be generous!

- Every day, reach out to several people and offer assistance.

- Help an elderly person to cross the street.

- Offer someone your help in the office.

- When you go out for dinner, leave a 25 percent tip every once in a while.

- Thank the waiter for his service and pass the compliment along to the manager.

- When you come home after work, hug your spouse, ask her about her day and really listen. Do not arrive in the house and start complaining about the misery or upsets you experienced during the day. This is called "dumping" and can come across as selfish and egocentric.

- After you have really listened to your spouse's concerns, you can ensure your own concerns and needs will be met later. When she opens up to you, curb your urge to give advice and direct her. She probably is not interested in hearing that. Just listen, ask some follow-up questions, or simply acknowledge what she is expressing.

- If you have children, spend some time sitting next to them and seeing what they have been up to. Be generous with your time and involvement. If they are drawing or creative in any way, resist any urges to correct or improve their work. Comment on the colors your child used and speak with enthusiasm about the creation, or ask your child to tell you a story about the process of producing it.

- At work, compliment your staff or fellow worker for their contribution. If you are a manager, go out of your way to publicly acknowledge someone for a job well done. Be generous with your customers. Find out what they are interested in and send them an article you come across that is for their interest. After an order has been filled or delivered, call your client or send a thank you note that expresses your appreciation and pleasure in your relationship with them.

EMPATHY

Susan

If you are like most people, you probably talk more than you listen.

Recently, Susan discussed a situation with me concerning a problem she was experiencing at work. She felt unfairly treated regarding her annual review. When she attempted to discuss it with her supervisor, she was met with a stern directive about the review and her bonus. She left her meeting feeling not listened to, much less empathized with. Feeling hurt and dismissed, she also felt fundamentally unvalued.

When she attempted to discuss what happened with her husband later that night, she was met with a great deal of his advice giving and direction. Although she told him she did not want any advice and some empathy would be helpful, her husband continued with increased advising and annoyance. She felt herself again feeling dismissed, so she told him to stop and withdrew into lonely silence.

Susan wanted empathy and acknowledgment of her feelings from both her supervisor and husband. In both situations, she felt sternly rebuked. What went wrong, she wondered? How did the conversation slip into frustration and distrust?

Both the manager and the husband missed the opportunity to empathize. If either had stopped directing and advising and simply acknowledged her disappointment, Susan would have felt heard and valued. Unfortunately, her husband responded in a way many men slip into when met with upset, frustration and disappointment. He gave advice.

Chances are he was trying to be helpful, thinking that his advice was an expression of empathy. Perhaps that was what he might want if he were having a difficult time. But in Susan's case, she needed him to acknowledge her hurt feelings, validate her emotional experience or put an arm around her as she began to open up. That would be the kind of empathy his wife needed.

LISTEN MORE AND TALK LESS

In my experience, talking is highly overvalued. Powerful listening goes a lot further in promoting a sense of well-being for others to feel valued and understood.

Unless your advice is requested, in most cases you will do more good by listening. You can always ask if the other person is open to some input and then express your thoughts. Ask if your comments are helpful. If not, stop talking, open your ears and listen some more.

When you empathize and listen, the Gorilla or Emotional Brain feels fed. Oxytocin, a powerful chemical, is secreted throughout the other person's body. There is a good chance you will experience the warm and tender sensations of oxytocin then being secreted in your own body. Her adrenaline and cortisol secretions will then be diminished, if not eliminated.

Not listening with empathy and giving unsolicited advice, especially spoken with a stern voice, are all life depleting.

Remember, the Gorilla Brain seeks to feel good, reduce pain and be more connected.

When upset is present, very little information gets into the thinking or Computer Brain. Bottom line: Stop giving advice and learn to give "bananas" instead.

TOUCH AND HUGS

When I was a young child growing up with an advice-giving, non-empathetic mother, I would sometimes walk over to my cousins' house. There, Honey or Ginger would sit me in her lap and read me a story. Very quickly, I would calm down as I felt a soft touch and heard a soft voice. I felt safe and loved. There was little talking, just sweet caring through touch and hugs. Within minutes, I would bounce off her lap and go about my business.

As a therapist, I sometimes touch a patient's hand or shoulder when he or she is in distress. I know it means a lot to them and I can see the appreciation in their eyes. In like fashion, perhaps through the action of mirror neurons, I also feel the warm energy in my body. After a session, I often walk down the hallway escorting a client with my arm around their shoulders and give a squeeze as we say goodbye. Especially after a tough session, the gesture goes a long way to promote a sense of safety and connection.

Vince Lombardi

There is a story about the legendary football coach, Vince Lombardi. After one particular game where the team lost, a player sat alone on a locker room bench with his face buried in his hands. He had missed a key pass and was feeling quite remorseful. All the other players were ignoring him or changing into their street clothes.

When Lombardi walked into the locker room, the silence was deafening. He was known for his temper and severe disciplining when displeased. He slowly walked over to the slumped over figure and sat close to him. Quietly he put his large and powerful arm around the player and said, "You've had a tough day. Tomorrow we'll work on your catching technique. We have a long season and other games to win."

That touch and kind words went a long way to soothe the player's disappointment in letting his team down. Lombardi knew that when a player felt down, a little tenderness was healing. He would save his discipline and anger for tomorrow on the practice field when he expected the player to learn from his mistakes.

A COLD STARE!

A number of years ago I attended a conference where a well-known psychiatrist was presenting. I liked what he was saying and wanted to contribute something back. I had recently been reading a book about loss and thought a brief comment about the book would add some value to the presentation. I was sitting in the front row with 400 others behind me. The facilitator, someone I knew, called on me. I stood and introduced myself and offered my contribution. I was met by the speaker's cold stare and total silence. I felt hurt, embarrassed and quietly dismissed.

I sat back down, thinking of all those colleagues behind me who were probably getting a laugh out of my situation. I felt the same way I did as a second grader at my piano recital. I could hardly wait for the morning session to end so I could make an exit.

As I sat and attempted to breathe deeply and soothe myself, I felt someone reach over and touch my shoulder. She simply said, "I liked your comments, thanks!"

That simple touch made all the difference. All my shame and sense of loneliness disappeared and I regained my confidence. I could literally feel the chemistry in my body shifting and re-energizing me.

I enjoyed the rest of the day. I was temporarily emotionally hijacked by the presenter's lack of connection. My colleague's touch sent a surge of positive energy through my body. It was wonderful to have a fellow gorilla reach out in such a kind and generous way.

EMOTIONAL MEMORIES

To this day, I am moved by memories of my second grade teacher soothing me, my cousin reading and holding me close and that colleague in the large auditorium reaching over to offer support. The memories flood me with gratefulness and gentle tears of appreciation. Like my fellow Gorillas, I feel connected and bonded knowing that I am cared for and valued. Whenever I am giving a talk or presentation, I think of those moments and I feel self-confidence growing inside of me.

We all need to feel connected, be it in real life or in our emotional memories. Take some time each day to reflect on your positive memories, the people you have met and enjoyed, and experiences that brought you pleasure. Linger on these gratifying memories as Rick Hanson suggests in his book *Hardwiring Happiness*.

He suggests remembering the experience and savoring it fully. Visualize it and see in your imagination what is happening. Evoke any sounds that might go along with the experience such as the sound of the ocean, wind rustling in the trees or the laughter of others. Take around 20 to 30 seconds to enjoy your imagery. In doing so, you are actually laying down new neural memory pathways for joy and pleasure.

Key Points

- You are emotional. Your brain has an appetite for feeling good, being connected to others and getting rid of pain.

- All mammals have a strong need to connect and bond.

- Infants who do not receive emotional connection often fail to thrive.

- Some ways to feed your emotional brain:
    - a) Sharing and generosity
    - b) Empathy and caring toward others
    - c) Listen more and talk less
    - d) Touching and hugging
    - e) Emotional memories

- Empathy and connections release oxytocin, the chemical cement for love and close relationships.

Chapter 20:

| FEEDING YOUR REPTILIAN BRAIN

Time to visit the oldest and most permanent of our three brains, the Survival Brain, also known as the Alligator or Reptilian Brain. The Alligator Brain never sleeps. Always alert to danger, it does not mind keeping you on edge if that will keep you safe. It is not as smart as its Computer neighbor or caring as the Emotional Brain. It has only one purpose: keeping you alive.

SURVIVAL

The Alligator Brain has not matured very much over the last 400 hundred million years. Your Computer and Gorilla Brains have developed and refined themselves so that you are now capable of perspective taking, problem solving, collaboration, cooperation and nurturing others. Yet, your Alligator Brain has been content to carry on as it has done since it began. In any given situation, if you can't quickly determine what is going on and mitigate something that is upsetting, your Alligator Brain might become agitated and stick its nose into your affairs. If it detects danger and threats to your safety, it has two response modes: fight or flight.

For example, Barbara's Alligator is fiercely loyal in this regard. Whenever her husband flirts or pays attention to another woman, she quickly jumps to the conclusion that he is planning to abandon her. Terrified, she accuses him of cheating, lying and planning to leave. Having experienced abandonment at an early age, she never developed the self-confidence or object constancy to appreciate that she is an attractive and smart adult and that it would be a foolish decision for her husband to leave.

Her reaction is instantaneous and intense, just as if she were still a defenseless child and that abandonment is only seconds away. In this situation, she is literally fighting for her life.

Barbara lacks object constancy, an ability to maintain a sense of emotional connection and safety even when temporarily upset or disappointed. She is unable to balance her terror of abandonment with the 20 years of caring and love her husband has given. She cannot nurture herself with those memories that he is a safe and caring partner who has shown a consistent connection. Unfortunately, the emotional hijack and descent down the slope toward despair is swift. The unconscious is always alert to danger, like a poisonous snake that has been struck and requires an immediate defensive reaction.

So, when anxiety intensifies, what can people like Barbara do to self-regulate and calm down?

SELF AWARENESS

First, Barbara can learn to recognize the tension rising in her body. She can learn to become aware of the sensations such as rapid heartbeat, shortness of breath and tension in her stomach. If she stays in her thoughts without paying attention to these other physical indicators, chances are she will jump to the catastrophic conclusion of abandonment and her terror will intensify. Instead, it is better to focus on her physical reactions.

Pausing, she can rate her bodily discomfort on a scale of 1-10, noticing where the tension is the strongest. If possible, she could also observe her thinking and write down her terrifying thoughts. The act of observing helps a person distance from the traumatic experience and better calibrate a workable solution. She also could remember earlier times when she felt hurt and defenseless and ask herself how she responded as a child. She can ask herself whether or not this is her preferred response now as an adult, or if there could be a more positive and powerful action she could take instead.

SELF REGULATION

Essentially, Barbara needs to take the time to hang out with her bodily symptoms. She could ask herself questions about her heartbeat:

If my heartbeat is a vehicle, what shape would it take? What color is it? How fast is it traveling?

If she says it feels like a speeding train, she could then visualize the train and describe its details such as exterior colors, number of cars and the sound it makes while speeding along the tracks. She could even imagine passengers sitting and working at their laptops or getting a bite to eat in the dining car. In this way, sometimes objectifying the sensations and being the observer can go a long way to instilling a greater sense of calmness and perspective. It enables the higher levels of cortical functioning to be allies for emotional recovery through imagination, guided imagery and distancing from emotional pain.

She could also breathe into her bodily reactions, meaning slow her breathing down and take 10-15 deep breaths. Deep breathing is not what we usually do when we are afraid. Yet, slow breathing activates the parasympathetic nervous system and elicits our relaxation response. As deep and slow breathing occur, the body begins to calm down and the more intense bodily reactions soften.

She also could also imagine a time when she felt cared for and safe. Her imagery could center on someone from her past or present. It might even be a pet such as a familiar dog or cat. Just imagining and visualizing such an experience of emotional connection can activate the Gorilla Brain and evoke a sense of protection and care. In response, the Alligator Brain can retreat back into its observer role and not push so hard.

One of the problems, as we have stated, is that the Alligator Brain does not distinguish between an imagined abandonment and a real one. For a given situation, the Alligator Brain does not want to take the time to include the Computer Brain to ascertain fact from fiction — that is too much of a risk, since the danger feels extremely real. Instead, the Alligator overreacts with its "better safe than sorry" approach, just in case the danger might be real and forthcoming.

SELF CARE

Barbara needs something else to help her to calm down. Perhaps a warm bath, some soothing music, reading or taking a walk. Too often anxiety can lead to overeating or drinking as a way to self soothe. While these methods can temporarily abate the discomfort, there is the possibility of addiction.

Exercise is another way to self-care for the body. As a person indulges in self-care, their adrenaline flow slows down. When that happens, one is more capable of thinking about how to better handle the fear, versus the "all or none" intense reaction triggered by the Alligator Brain.

GRATITUDES

Some people use gratitude as a way to self-regulate. They take a few deep breaths and then think about everything for which they are grateful. For example, every day on my way to work, I notice when tension rises in my body.

I take some deep breaths and then recite out loud everything for which I offer gratitude: my wife, children, patients and friends.

Taking in the full richness of my life, I also express gratitude for my career, creativity, health, resiliency, curiosity, and many others. My tension usually drops away and I feel more alert, looking forward to my day.

Gratitudes are very powerful. Ask yourself: "For what am I grateful today?" and take the time to reflect on the pleasure and appreciation you are feeling.

REFRAMING
Another strategy is to ask yourself, "Is there any other way I can look at this situation other than taking it so personally?"

Coming up with several other options or explanations broadens your perspective and can even generate problem solving. It is an excellent idea for stepping out of your mental and emotional rut to look more freshly at the situation.

During a session with Barbara, she began to slip into catastrophic thinking about her husband abandoning her. They had been out to dinner the night before when she noticed her husband looking away from her. Her immediate explanation was that he was looking at his mistress.

I distracted her by asking her to stand and shake off some tension, take several deep breaths and sing "Happy Birthday" to me in a loud voice.

She then sat down and I asked her to come up with four other explanations for her husband's distraction.

She came up with the following: he saw a business associate, he was having a stroke, he was looking for the waitress to signal her to bring an "I love you" cake to the table and lastly, he had to pass gas.

She laughed. We then explored the underlying belief system that was keeping her catastrophic thinking alive and thriving.

IT'S NOT PERSONAL

Let's face it! If you are like most people, you probably take most things personally. You might say "not so," but I do not believe you. Humans tend to easily feel hurt, excluded, criticized, made fun of, ignored, taken advantage of, not appreciated, misunderstood, lied to, manipulated and talked down to.

The truth is you really are not that important except to a select kinship group. Remember, people do not wake up each day thinking about how to make your day difficult. They are just too preoccupied with surviving their day and wondering who is out to get them.

Taking things personally is a reflection of your Alligator or Survival Brain taking life too seriously. Get over it and chalk it up to being thin-skinned. Be creative and give others the benefit of the doubt. Try to be generous and kind. If you take things too personally, you will attract more and more perceived slights, slings and arrows in your life. Eventually, all you will have is personal misery, hurt feelings and others thinking that you are just a jerk.

Then you will be right about taking things personally because you created it to be that way. You have created your own "emotional allergy" and get upset each time you personalize or self-reference someone's behavior. Doing so, you constantly get thrown down the slope of emotional disintegration, feeding your Wolf of Evil and spending wasted time in your Death Psychology.

A potential remedy is to simply ask the person something like, "Is it your intention to make me feel stupid, unattractive and inadequate, or am I just being over-sensitive and taking this too personally?"

This question gets you out of your head and into communication.

A MIGHTY FORCE

The Alligator Brain is a mighty force that works diligently to protect you. Unfortunately, it is still looking for lions, wild baboons, poisonous snakes and other predators that might do us harm. It is still acting and reacting like we are living in the jungle and surrounded by enemy elements. Eighty percent of the time, 2,000 thoughts a day and 50 bothersome stresses are its roaming grounds.

No wonder it is hypersensitive to danger. It needs constant soothing from the Computer and Gorilla Brains to back off and calm down. Alligators do not make good pets and they snap too easily. Keep them under control.

Key Points

- The Reptilian Brain never sleeps and is always vigilant to signs of danger or harm.

- The Reptilian Brain is your Survival Brain.

- The Reptilian brain has an appetite for:
    - a) Self-awareness
    - b) Self-regulation and calming down
    - c) Self-care
    - d) Gratitude
    - e) Reframing situations from dangerous to challenging
    - f) Not taking things so personally

- Feed it what it wants and become an Alligator Tamer.

Chapter 21:

WHAT IS THE VALUE OF FEEDING THE TRIUNE BRAIN?

If you have three children and they do not get what they want, how might they behave? Would they simply say "no problem, I can wait" or would they stomp around, sulk and throw a tantrum?

Like your children, the three parts of your brain want to be fed and taken care of. Treat them well and they will be of great service to you. Ignore or take advantage of them and they will get you back. If you are aware, thoughtful, considerate and also able to set limits with your Computer, Gorilla and Alligator, how might they return the value to you?

WHAT DO PEOPLE WANT?

When it comes down to it, how do you answer the question "What do people want?"

Do you want wealth, friendship, love, control, success, admiration, respect, knowledge, mastery, ability, domination, fellowship, teamwork, being left alone, creativity, time to reflect, fun, recreational time, sexual satisfaction, novelty, etc.? There are so many to choose from. Some might have higher value than others, but all of us want and desire something.

When we get what we want it feels good, at least for a while until another appetite or desire pulls us into action.

All your dreams and desires can probably be subsumed under three umbrellas: Power, Connection and Safety, the three major appetites of your Computer, Gorilla and Alligator Brains. Rick Hanson suggests these needs as Satisfaction, Connection and Safety.

When you look into your vision and reflect on what you really want, one or more of these desires will probably beckon to you.

Let's say, for example, you envision being rich sometime in the future. This might be a desire for power, love or safety. If you have enough money, you might assume you can control and have anything you want. This is, after all, what power is about. Or perhaps money will buy you affection and love and provide proof that you are lovable and cared for. Hence your desire for connection will be satisfied. Then again, wealth may offer you a protection against scarcity and vulnerability, so safety might be the object of your vision.

You stand a better chance of breaking into your zone of success and satisfaction if you are already feeling powerful, connected and safe. It might pay, then, to feed these basic Triune needs early on rather than striving hard to gain them in the future. Your future quest may be a reflection of scarcity and not a true vision at all.

Remember the power of your Reptilian Brain. Danger is pervasive. The Gorilla or Alligator may be pushing you into a desperate pursuit of an endless quest. You may want your Computer Brain to figure out how you can feed and satisfy these needs on a more immediate and daily basis so you can get on with living an extraordinary life.

If you are regularly feeding your "hungry children," that may free up your curiosity and energy to pursue a more engaging and nourishing vision such as living an extraordinary life of creativity or generosity, of service or contribution to a larger benefit other than your personal hunger for Power, Connection or Safety. They all may be closer than you think; maybe right around the corner if your eyes and other senses are open to discover them.

INVESTING YOUR RESOURCES

Navigators for success use their resources wisely. They do not choose to live their lives at a cost. They aim to invest their resources for a maximal ROI. They value using Power, Connection and Safety each day in order to create visions worth having. Their Breakthrough Thinking centers around feeding their hungry brains, quieting their anxieties and using their higher frequency energies to move toward any rewarding future they so envision. They aim to not get swallowed up in the competition for their resources. They use their personal resources to think differently, operating outside the box, allowing their creativity and higher-level energy frequencies to propel them into the Breakthrough Zone. Here is where you can savor the sweet taste of immortal living.

POSSIBILITY

Leonardo da Vinci imagined realities not attainable in the 16th century. Airplanes. Submarines. Helicopters. He saw life through uncensored eyes. He did not censor his imagination with limiting thoughts such as "it's unrealistic," or "I can't make a living out of this" or "people will think I'm crazy." He imagined these possibilities and drew them into existence for others in later centuries to figure out the details. He was a futurist.

James Watts in the 18th century created the steam engine. It was up to future builders to use these insights to build the railroad, the internal combustion engine, cars, airplanes and space rockets. He was a futurist who was captured by an idea and a possibility.

Martin Luther King had a dream that transformed a culture and led to the election of an African-American President.

President Kennedy in 1960 said we would land on the moon and return safely within a decade when there was no scientific reality at the time for such a vision. He left it to others to figure out the operational application of his vision.

There are researchers now who have been able to take a person's thoughts, feelings and visual images and transmit them electronically across thousands of miles into the brains of others who have similar electrodes. Perhaps these individuals are the arbiters of future mental telepathy, mind travel and astral projection.

These are creative minds at work opening visions and new vistas that invite others to enhance and fulfill into reality. Perhaps this is the ultimate Breakthrough Thinking; the evolution of a generous mind connected to other minds, all committed to a future worth having, not one based in scarcity and fear. Consider what could be accomplished with Computers, Gorillas and Alligators all being cared for so that one community of brains, 100 billion neurons, can work together in unison to create visions not yet imagined.

This may be too far out to digest. Maybe it is a pipe dream. We will eventually see. In the meantime, feed your brain and create greater peace of mind, health and even longevity to enjoy. Play with outrageous visions. Who knows where each of you will lead us in our jointly held desire to live extraordinary long lives of success, accomplishment and satisfaction. Even if we do not fulfill our visions, enjoy the wonderful journey of not playing it safe.

In the next chapter, we will explore how Life Navigators think about their lives and what they do to take care of and feed their three brains.

Key Points

- If you neglect feeding and caring for your Computer, Gorilla and Alligator Brains, they will make your life difficult until you pay attention to them.

- The Computer, Gorilla and Alligator Brains are like three children. They want what they want and they do not like waiting or being ignored.

- Your integrated brain thrives on a mixture of Power, Connection and Safety.

- When well-fed, your integrated brain will support Breakthrough Thinking.

- Breakthrough thinking saves you energy, time and other valuable resources that you can then use to invest in generating a great life, rather than squandering it as you slide down the slope into resentment, despair and personal disintegration.

Chapter 22:

THE ART OF LIFE NAVIGATION

There are about six billion people on the planet. Somehow, we all get through life. Some fare better than others. We are all driven or guided by an invisible force, an internal GPS of which most people are unaware. If you become aware of this force or energy and learn how to pay attention to it, you can use it as a resource for a personal breakthrough.

On the other hand, if you are not attentive to your internal energies or rhythms, you become a Victim to its power. Rather than recognizing and working with this powerful force, Victims slip into the downward spiral of life toward inflammation and eventual despair, thus reducing their chances toward achieving longevity.

THE NAVIGATORS

Navigators have an advantage compared to Survivors and Victims. They seem to do a better job of feeding their logical, emotional and survival brains — including the Wolf of Love — and using Breakthrough Thinking to live successful, accomplished and highly satisfying lives. Navigators do not take things for granted. Recognizing and appreciating what they have to deal with in their lives they strive to create and cope with life's demands. They also declare and chart their own life course, learning along the way how to succeed. At the same time, they take care of their inner world in terms of self-regulation. Realizing that they need their brains, minds and bodies to support them in their pursuit of success and happiness, they take care of their bodies and energy. They become masters of rewiring and evolving their brains.

YOUR GPS

Navigators have a sense of what guides them to living a great life. They have a map or GPS to help orient them as they move through their lives. Like all human beings, they have to deal with life's frustrations, disappointments and traumas, but at some point in their life cycle they break through into the world of navigation.

The GPS is both external and internal. Navigators spend time thinking about and designing a plan to move from their current situation toward their desired visions and goals. They strive to understand their internal world and how their brains function. They constantly work on both enhancing life-sustaining thinking and reducing whatever self-limiting beliefs and self-destructive behaviors can get in the way of living a joyful and enduring life.

In the external world, Navigators ask and answer the four key questions:

What do they want to accomplish?

Why is this important to them?

Who do they have to be to succeed?

How do they have to rewire their brains?

They may use a formula to keep themselves focused and on track. Perhaps the formula might be something like:

Success = Passion + Goals + Actions + Resiliency

Their internal dialogue consists of:

What do I really love in life and what do I want to accomplish?

What specific actions can I take each day to move closer to my dream?

When breakdowns or upset occur, how can I bounce back?

They know what they want and what is in their hearts, set specific targets to shoot for, choose key actions to take on a daily basis and keep learning and bouncing back with resilience when confronting problems.

NAVIGATIONAL COMPETENCE

To succeed, Navigators develop competence in a number of key areas. These competencies are like the tools in a carpenter's toolbox, and they use them as the situation requires.

A master carpenter is selective in the tools he uses. For example, a saw is ideal for cutting, a ruler for measuring, a screwdriver for screws, and a hammer for pounding nails. Would it not be a foolish and poor practice to just grab any tool close by? Why use a hammer to cut wood or a saw to pound nails? The Navigator thinks like the master carpenter.

Navigators first work to design their maps to create Breakthrough Thinking and then use their tools appropriately to fit the situation. Let's now look at the tools in the Navigator's Toolkit. Some are Power Tools, some Connection Tools and others are Safety Tools.

THE NAVIGATOR'S TOOLKIT

SELF AWARENESS

"I know what I am thinking and feeling. I am aware of my strengths and weaknesses."

Without self-awareness, nothing much can change. Navigators take the time to notice what is going on in their lives. What's happening between people? Sensing discomfort or a break in trust, they think about the event, feeling or situation and work to get back on track.

They notice their thinking and feeling patterns.

They know their strengths and weaknesses.

They even appreciate how they may be the one creating a difficult time when things break down.

Bringing an open mindset to life allows them to see, hear and experience the full spectrum of events in their lives. Open-mindedness and self-awareness are the foundation stones of taking responsibility and choosing the right actions. Navigators rely heavily on these basic skills and continually use them to stay focused and on course.

Jim

Jim, a 48-year-old CEO and entrepreneur, is a take-charge kind of guy. As a very successful entrepreneur, he is action-oriented, quick to respond and would rather ask for forgiveness than ask for permission. Although sometimes he may choose strategies that fail, he is quick to recognize his own impulsive nature and works to get back on track. When anxious, he tends to be a blamer and directive kind of person, not always cooperative or collaborative. He has come to recognize these tendencies and is working on toning down his controlling behaviors.

He now knows that a surge of anxiety or stress often underlies his take-charge style. Because he is aware and open to feedback from others, he has broken out of a survival mode into one of navigation.

Now, he spends more time in Breakthrough Thinking rather than in breakdown mode. He also has grown to understand the havoc and resentment he creates when occasionally slipping into his default blaming and controlling behavior patterns.

Jim has come to understand how he had been creating relationship crises, distrust and avoidant reactions in others. Now that he is getting older and sees the value of creating safety and connection with others, he is applying his strong entrepreneurial style to anticipate how his behavior might demotivate others less driven than himself. By paying attention to how others feel, he is learning to ride the navigational wave of connection, then using more participatory rather than directive ways to influence others.

VISIONARY THINKING
"I am passionate and know what I want to accomplish!"

Wayne Gretzky, a legendary hockey player, was known to say when asked about his ability to anticipate and score, "I skate where the puck is going, not where it already is." Navigators skate to where they are going.

They look into the future and aim to succeed, setting their sights on challenging targets and perhaps not initially knowing what they are doing. It is not unusual for Navigators to fail several times before they get on the right track, learn the right skills and draw in the right resources. Others might think of them as unrealistic dreamers. They probably are but they don't waste much time anguishing about what others think about them. They are too engrossed in their visions and adventures.

Thomas Edison envisioned creating an electric light bulb. He tried thousands of experiments, some say almost 10,000 before succeeding. He did not give up.

I imagine there were many times he felt discouraged and wondered if the effort was worth it. But he persevered in transforming his dream into a reality. He learned along the way and now his vision lights up the world.

A friend of mine, Sam Katz, ran unsuccessfully for mayor of Philadelphia several times. He was a Republican and the last Republican mayor elected was Richardson Dilworth in the 1950s. I once asked him about his thought process and why he kept chasing his "Impossible Dream" in the face of such consistent failure. He pondered the question for a moment and then answered, "Delusional! You have to be a bit delusional to keep your dreams going."

The good news is that Sam indeed lived his vision of "servant leadership" by providing value and contributing to the city he loved, but not as mayor. Instead, he has successfully created the first documentary movie on the history of his beloved city.

As a football coach, Dick Vermeil had a dream to win the Super Bowl. Although he brought the Philadelphia Eagles to the pinnacle of success in the early 1980s, his team lost their bid for the championship. After the loss, Dick was devastated and exhausted. He left football and channeled his abundant energies elsewhere. Although very successful for the next decade, he still longed for his vision of Super Bowl victory.

Ten years later, in his 60s, when most coaches retire, he took on the task of coaching the St. Louis Rams, a losing team with a record of three wins, and 13 losses. His dream re-ignited with this new opportunity and, armed with a new awareness of his strengths and weaknesses, he applied himself to pursue his dream. Three years later, he stood in triumph, holding the Super Bowl Championship Trophy high above his head to the applause and appreciation of tens of thousands of fans.

Maybe he, Sam Katz and Thomas Edison all had something in common: powerful visions and a touch of delusional thinking. I consider them excellent examples of navigational thinking and riding the wave of change with power, connection and self-expression. All experienced stressful life situations that called for Breakthrough Thinking. They were able to break out of their shells of reactivity, fear and discouragement, and launch into their respective breakthrough zones of success and personal fulfillment.

RESULTS ORIENTATION
"I know what I want and how to execute!"

Navigators aim to get things done. They tend to be thoughtful about what is important and take actions that lead them toward their goals. Taking on challenges, they focus on what they are doing. Consequently, they are more successful than Survivors and Victims because they do not waste excessive time in actions that are unproductive or irrelevant to their vision. They are very capable of relaxing and having fun but, when push comes to shove, they get back on task and keep the end in sight so they are in a better position to make the right choices. They practice Pareto's Law: doing the 20 percent of activities that provide 80 percent of the results.

A recent client of mine had always wanted to run his own business. He worked in a family business owned by his in-laws. As stubborn controllers, both of the owners were attached to doing business the way they had been for years.

My client saw opportunities to take the company to a national level and expand its market. Although facing severe resistance from his father-in-law, who was fighting to maintain his territorial control, my client stayed focused and results-oriented. He took on the national market and fought his way to success through technological breakthroughs and exceptional customer service. To gain credibility and respect in his industry, he achieved an MBA degree, even though he never received an undergraduate degree. In fact, in the history of the college, he was the first non-degree student accepted. He was unstoppable because he was results-oriented.

Today, he is president of his company.

He channeled his anxiety, tough-mindedness and aggressions into "skating to where the puck was going" and taking actions that moved his teams and company forward. Still plagued at times by anxiety and a dominating personality, he is starting to explore how to enhance his sense of safety and connection with others. He has not yet caught this navigational wave of change but is exploring its possibilities.

RESPONSIBILITY
"I take responsibility for everything I do and what happens to me!"

Navigators do not make excuses or blame others. They take responsibility for their lives, actions and choices. They work to figure out what went wrong and rewire their approach to tackling challenges. When they make a mistake or fail, they take little time in blaming themselves or in feeling shame. They strive to understand the breakdown and make the necessary improvements. This is an essential Breakthrough Thinking skill since failures are frequent when you are playing outside your comfort zone, playing for big stakes and taking on challenges.

Ralph was an investment banker who wanted to be an entrepreneur. He knew nothing about how to think or act like an entrepreneur, but that was his vision. Terrified of stepping out of his comfort zone, he had to learn a great deal and accomplish much rewiring to succeed. A perfectionist and detail-oriented person by nature, Ralph had to learn a new set of entrepreneurial attitudes, strategies and practices. He spent the next seven years fumbling in his dream, often falling on his face and bumbling his way from one mistake to another. His banker colleagues often teased him and urged him to be more "responsible" and act like an adult.

Partnering up with a successful entrepreneur, he slowly learned the ropes. Today, he is a multimillionaire and respected by his colleagues, staff and other entrepreneurs. He took responsibility for his path, choices, mistakes and eventual successes. He stayed the course and rode through the wave of change with the help of his navigating partner. He stayed true to his passion even in the face of considerable failure and social criticism from those who had chosen to stay in their traditional roles. Now he mentors other entrepreneurs.

CONNECTION & EMPATHY
"I care about others and my relationships!"

Navigators appreciate their emotional connections with others. When others are troubled, they empathize. They do not rush in with advice or bring up the topic of their own troubles. They just keep their stories to themselves and focus on their partner. They also check in with key people during the day saying, "I've been thinking about you and wanted to connect. How are you doing? Anything you want to share with me?" Or they connect by text or Facebook to share an experience with them.

Connection releases oxytocin, a hormone that creates a warm, pleasurable emotion in the body. With oxytocin, people thrive. Without it, they shrink inside.

Navigators tend to be emotional listeners, powerfully reaching to the essence of the other person's experience. They listen with their heart and are open to understanding and appreciating someone else's personal experience.

THE EMPATHY PROCESS

Many Navigators practice a three-step empathy process: understanding, validating, and empathizing.

Joey, 17, was struggling with choosing what to pursue in his life. College was one option, but he was also pulled toward doing volunteer missionary work with his church in South America. Noticing that Joey was struggling over his dilemma, his father took a chance to connect with him. "You seem to be struggling a lot lately," he said. "Anything I can help you with?"

"No, Dad, but thanks anyway. It's my problem and I have to figure out what I should do when I graduate high school this year."

"Sounds like you're having a mental tug-of-war between some choices."

"Yeah, I really don't know what to do. I want a college education, but also feel pulled to go to the mission in South America for my next year."

"I can appreciate your struggle. You value a college education, but do not want to miss out on this opportunity to contribute. I know that both are important to you."

"Thanks, Dad, yeah, you got it right. I am torn and a bit confused right now."

"I imagine you might be feeling some uncertainty and anxiety about making the right choice. Am I right?"

"Yeah, I do feel confused. Do I sound crazy to you?"

"You do not sound crazy to me. In fact, you make a lot of sense. You're pulled in two directions and are feeling confused. Would it help to talk it through for a while?"

Joey was struggling with an internal conflict and was stuck. His dad, rather than trying to convince his son to go to college and perhaps later travel to work at the mission, simply tried to understand his son's thinking, acknowledge his feelings, and validate his thinking. Joey felt valued and appreciated his father's empathetic concerns. After several similar conversations, Joey came to the decision to go to college, and then spend his summer vacation at the mission. I think their Wolves of Love got connected in a way that most fathers and sons never realize.

LISTENING
"It is a gift to listen!"

We talk too much!

Talking is vastly overrated. We talk to make an impression, thinking that others really care about what we have to say.

Wrong!

People want to be heard and seen. Listening is the gift of intimate caring. When you listen, the person experiences a sense of being valued and appreciated. They then feel safer with you and might even trust you more. So, if you want to feel important, give the gift of importance to others. They will value you for your generosity.

Try talking 30 percent of the time and listening 70 percent. The ROI on listening is immense. You end up with a sense of increased safety, trust and connection. The other person might even then ask you what you think.

SAFETY
"We all need a safe harbor!"

June, a 43-year-old patient, suffered from severe anxiety and distress, and was easily buffeted by minor disappointments and frustrations. She also was experiencing an obsessive preoccupation with what a failure her life had become.

As a young child, June had never felt safe in the world; she experienced severe separation anxiety and panic when her parents were not close at hand. Her dependency on them was great and she continually relied on them to "rescue" her from any problem she was experiencing.

Throughout childhood, she tended to be a loner, forming only fragile connections with others and easily hurt when others did not gratify her demands.

As a teenager, life for June did not improve. She continued to be frightened, insecure and incapable of self-regulating her emotions or coping with her school or social lives.

Each time she ran into a problem, she would panic and demand her parents step in to rescue her.

June grew up never learning to successfully cope with reality or calm herself down when emotionally upset. She had very poor self-regulatory skills and continued to be highly reactive to minor upsets. She functioned as if she had "second degree emotional burns:" highly sensitive to upsets and taking no responsibility for her situation.

June was a very difficult and resistant patient, someone who continually felt victimized by life and overwhelmed by daily stresses. She only began to experience safety input when we spent considerable time learning to calm down her nervous system and to self-soothe. Working with her proved to be very difficult and stressful. It was like trying to control a runaway train speeding down a mountainside without knowing where the brakes were located.

Our work focused on self-regulatory training, resiliency coaching and finding small patches of things to appreciate in a life of her own perceived storms, tsunamis and hurricanes. It is very hard, if not impossible, to experience a life of vitality, health and self-expression when a person lives in a state of fear and survival. Thinking alone usually is insufficient to pull us out of this psychological state of dread and tension.

The self-regulatory, self-caring and resiliency actions seem to do a better job in calming down our over active and over-heated psyches.

Self Regulation
"I know how to pace myself and cool down."

When I was a teenager, I got my first car. I think it was a 1952 Chevy, stick shift. It had a radiator filled with water, which served as the coolant. It was not unusual for my car to overheat on warm days, particularly if I aimed to climb over Clinton Mountain on my way to visit relatives. As the temperature gauge inched upward toward the boiling point, I would pull over, lift the hood and gently remove the radiator cap to allow the car to cool down.

Like that car, our bodies are prone to over-heating. Stress, lack of sleep, worry and anger all serve to increase our internal temperatures and edge us closer and closer to boiling over. We can over heat to the point of having a heart attack, inflammation, a panic attack or severe physical breakdowns. Think of the expression "Heart Attack!"

It sounds like something has invaded your body's immune system and attacked your heart. It is really heart failure, but in our culture perhaps we are more comfortable with the notion of physical breakdowns due to an attack rather than a failure.

Navigators are aware of over-heating and breaking down. They have learned to listen to their bodies to inform themselves about their internal stress. They try to pace themselves, pause and take breaks to self-regulate.

Every once in a while, perhaps two hours into a task, they stop and take some deep breaths, stretch, take a walk or talk to a friend. They may gaze out of a window into the distance, letting their imaginations take them to a faraway seashore or vacation site. This open gazing relaxes the body, especially if you take time to actually see what you are looking at. In this way, they are practicing Recovery Time, allowing their nervous system to cool down and to regain focus.

Navigators know the value of cooling down and self-regulating. They seek a long and healthy life. Overheat and you will break down, maybe even die.

They realize there is nothing to prove. Life is not a race! No need to be heroic in the workplace. Navigators do not push to climb the hill. When necessary, they pull over and cool down.

June was not a Navigator. She was a Victim on her way to being a Survivor. Easily stressed and over-heated, she was prone to catastrophic thinking and emotional flooding.

When she came in for her sessions, it was necessary to spend the first 20 minutes calming her down by teaching her how to be present in my office and be focused on our work together, rather than slipping into her usual panic and galloping narrative of overwhelm. Truthfully, these 20-minute grounding exercises in self-regulation were as much for me as for her!

Self-regulation was achieved by slowing down the speed of her breathing and shifting from shallow throat breathing to abdominal breathing. Also, noticing where her tension was trapped in her body helped. She seemed particularly responsive to EFT, tapping on various acupressure points to release energy blocks. She particularly liked and responded to the experience of "state changes" in her body and mind when I would coach her through guided imagery experiences where she would see herself in a future state feeling safe and relaxed. At such times, her body would calm down. She would breathe deeply and slowly. A smile of pleasure would appear. Gradually, she learned to use guided imagery and the breathing exercises during the day when she would grant herself recovery breaks.

RESILIENCY

"I don't give up! I learn from my mistakes, adapt and try again."

Anything worth doing has a good chance of failure. Navigators look forward to failure because that is when they learn what is not working. Rather than feeling defeated, they think about what happened, refresh themselves, consider what to do and get back into action. They bounce back with renewed energy and application of their talents and skills. Failure, renewal and refocused action are their formula for success.

Tracy Austin

Tracy Austin, a successful tennis star, knew something about resilience. After every point, won or lost, she would quickly turn her back to the net and slowly walk back to the baseline. It took her about 30 seconds to reach baseline. In that time, she slowed her breathing and heart rate by 30 percent. By the third set, she had more than a 30 percent energy reserve to draw on to defeat her opponents.

Tracy knew something about resilience combined with self-regulation. Do you pause, pull off the road and re-energize like Tracy and my old car, or do you push on and exhaust yourself trying to live up to an unrealistic expectation? Navigators preserve energy and live longer and healthier lives.

Over time, June and I worked on building up her resiliency. Once reasonably calmed down, we would venture into a recent upset and attempt to discuss it as if she were observing a movie of herself, telling me what she noticed. Every once in a while, we would pause and check her stress level and bodily reactions. The goal was to teach her how to self-regulate and gradually revisit her upsets.

Over time, she became more resilient and better able to talk about her experiences and not get emotionally hijacked. It was like teaching a foreigner a new language or taking someone with brain damage through an emotional rehabilitation program.

GRATITUDE AND SELF-ACKNOWLEDGMENT
"Sometimes you need a pat on the back!"

An excellent practice for enhanced living and peace of mind is to give gratitude. Every day before you begin your day, take a deep breath and give five Gratitudes. Think of someone really important to you and be grateful for your relationship.

Then think of someone else and again experience the warmth of being grateful.

Next, imagine yourself as a young child and express gratitude to yourself.

Remember someone who died and contributed to your life.

Lastly, express gratitude to yourself.

Indulge yourself in each gratitude. See, hear and feel the person you are caring about and honoring. Like a pleasant aroma, breathe in the experience. Your body with all its complex neural connections and your trillions of cells will all appreciate the snack.

You might even start a Victory Log. Each day, jot down several things you did that day that you feel good about. Perhaps it was an act of generosity and caring, a completed project, fulfilling a promise or making a difficult phone call. Your victories do not have to be big, just little acts of navigation to activate a dose of dopamine or endorphins to your brain and nervous system.

With practice and much support, June learned to express gratitude and appreciation for what was going on in her life, such as her new friendships, success at work, learning self-care and coping skills, and love for her child.

Through emotional connection and bonding with her child, June was finally able to find value and love in a relationship. She was subsequently able to use this connection to continue growing up and finding more safety and peace in her life. While never traveling into the world of the Navigator, June had learned how to survive.

BELIEF MANAGEMENT

As we have said, beliefs are physical and impact your body. Positive and life enhancing beliefs bathe the body's cells and proteins in life-generating neurotransmitters and hormones. Negative beliefs lead to secretions of adrenaline and cortisol and, eventually, cell breakdown, immunological weakness and illness.

By sustaining positive beliefs and actions, the Alligator Brain does not have to work so hard, thereby giving the Computer and Gorilla Brains more opportunities to work together for our health and well-being.

RUN LIKE A SPRINTER

Humans are not designed to be marathon runners. We do best working for short periods of time, around 90 minutes, then taking a recovery break. Working more than this amount of time wears people down and decreases their ability to focus, problem solve and collaborate.

The great tennis champion Tracy Austin practiced the "run like a sprinter" strategy. She had an exceptionally high third-set win percentage, often defeating stronger players when there was a tie. Her strategy: to fight for every point. Once won or lost, she would turn her back to the net and slowly walk back to baseline. In the 30 seconds it took her to get back, her respiratory and cardiovascular rates would drop by 30 percent. That technique gave her an edge that the other player did not have.

Her strategy was similar to track runners who run the 100-yard dash. While they run full out during each trial, they would then spend considerable time in recovery, rebuilding their energy reserves.

This translates to a person's workplace, where you work like a sprinter for about 90 minutes and then take a recovery break for 15 minutes. Research suggests that such a routine results in residual energy reserves late in the afternoon, around 4:00 pm, which is normally a time when energy reserves drop. Like Tracy Austin, if you practice her "run like a sprinter" strategy, you too will experience a reserve of energy when others begin to falter.

There they are, nine life practices you can use to rewire your brain for optimal performance, health and life extension. The more you practice these breakthrough competencies, the stronger and healthier you will become. Neurons that fire together get wired together.

Life Navigators use these practices to move into Breakthrough Performance and life enhancement. It is not magic or luck. They succeed by observing, pausing, self-renewing and staying focused on their visions. They know that distractions and wasted worry kill off dreams, success and life. Focused action, clear direction, self-regulation and Gratitudes heal and sustain life.

Key Points

- If you do not manage your internal GPS effectively, negativity and anxiety increase and life becomes a cost rather than an investment.

- Navigators value and pay attention to their internal GPS systems. They strive to discover ways to nurture and strengthen the appetites for Power, Connection and Safety.

- Navigators ask themselves four key questions in their pursuit of living extraordinary lives:
    1) What do I want to accomplish?
    2) Why is this important?
    3) Who do I have to be to succeed?
    4) How do I have to rewire my brain?

- Navigators have a success formula
  Success = Passion, Goals, Action and Resiliency

- "I know what is important to me, what targets I am working toward, what actions will get me there and how to bounce back when I fail."

- Navigators develop and enhance key tools and competencies for success
    a) **Power Tools**
      1. Self-awareness
      2. Visionary thinking and goal setting
      3. Results orientation

4. Responsibility

5. Coping skills

6. Creativity and discovery

b) **Connection Tools**

1. Empathy

2. Listening

3. Close connections with others

4. Relationship with oneself

5. Hugs and touching

6. Showing appreciation toward others

c) **Safety Tools**

1. Slow, deep breathing

2. Positive future imagery

3. Meditation and mindfulness

4. Self-regulation and cooling down
the nervous system

5. Resiliency and bouncing back

6. Belief management

7. Exercise

8. "Run like a sprinter" living

Chapter 23

REGRETS, GRIEVANCES AND LOST OPPORTUNITIES

DEATH PSYCHOLOGY

Life has a structure. Until recent times everyone has been limited by this structure. You are born, spend a short period of time going through life and then you die. No one has yet broken out of this structure. We all live in a "Death Psychology" in which the final result is still death, regardless of what we do. There has not been any magic potion to save us from this Death Psychology.

Some have played the game well with class, humor or pride. Others have stumbled about accumulating possessions to temporarily recharge their psychic batteries. Some become addicted to substances, temper or pain. Some have even chosen to cheat Fate by taking their own lives.

Here's how I view the situation. For a number of decades, all of us — you, me and everyone else — are on the playing field of life. Some get to play it for nearly 80 years, while others drop out much earlier. For a few, life continues until 100 years but not usually in good health.

In any case, regardless of our age at death, our lifetimes seem too short and we wonder how the time went by so fast.

Perhaps life ended by accident, illness or disaster. If the endgame is death, the final score is the same for everyone. However it happens, you end up sidelined from the playing field of life never to play again. The game is over!

There is good news, though. It looks like the structure of the game is going to change for the better. According to writers such as David Kekich, author of the book *Smart, Strong and Sexy, At 100?* (2012) and researchers such as Dr. Aubrey DeBrey and Dr. Bill Andrews, science and technology will soon introduce us to a longer time in the game of life, one with less illness and perhaps a reversal of the aging process.

Wouldn't that be great, not to worry about being sidelined and out of life? The game may go on for 150, 250 years or even longer.

For the present time though, we are all still living under the threat and inevitability of death. Many people I come in contact with spend considerable time in worry, anxiety, regret and disappointment. They lament over the choices they have made or are jealous that others seem to be doing better.

Some think if they could just make more money or have a better house, then they will feel successful, be smarter, taller or more attractive, have better friends or family.

All of us are experimenters, trying one thing or another to live a safe and maybe even an extraordinary life. It seems that searching for happiness in external riches or success does not work for most people in the long run. Life runs its course swiftly and sooner or later all of us have a look at how our lives turned out.

When close to death, many look back with sadness and wish for a little more time. When people who are close to death are interviewed, they often express a number of common regrets.

Perhaps these regrets provide some insights into what you can do earlier in life to take better control of your life outcomes down the road.

THE FIVE REGRETS OF THE DYING

According to Bronnie Ware, author of *The Top Five Regrets of the Dying* (2012), a book based on eight years of caring for and interviewing people close to death, five consistent regrets are reported.

1. **"I wish I had the courage to have lived my life true to myself rather than trying to live up to the expectations of others."**

They wished they had done their own thing and were less worried about what others thought or expected. Rather than asserting themselves and standing up for their own desires and choices, they mostly went along with what they thought others wanted. In the end, they regretted it. They lived reactive lives and ending up aching for the opportunities they had allowed to pass them by.

» Are you living the life that you dreamed of? Or are you worried and preoccupied by what others want and expect?

It takes courage to point your direction, walk your path and figure out how to succeed. Most people do not go this route, choosing instead to fit in and not make waves.

» Are you a wave maker or a fitter-in kind of person?

Life Navigators make waves and learn to ride them along the way. In the process, they get stronger, more flexible and resilient.

2. "I wish I did not work so hard!"

Do you ever hear a small voice whispering to you, "Go home!" or "Say no!" or "Let someone else do it!" Have you ever heard: "Turn off the phone and just take a walk"?

Navigators know how to say no. Even when they enjoy or love their work, they step away and take some recovery time. They know the drill of "run like a sprinter."

Life is not a marathon and there is no place to get to. Navigators call a time out. They catch their breath and, in the process, earn the art of living a balanced life, sometimes working hard and long and other times excusing themselves and dropping out. It all depends on which appetite needs attention. Work does not always come first, but to develop the art of choice requires letting go of figuring the whole thing out and thinking in black and white ways.

Life Navigators are aware of their varied appetites and realize that trying to sequence things perfectly results in rigidity and not extraordinary living.

3. The third regret is "Not expressing one's feelings."

Many people believe it is better to suppress and keep your feelings to yourself. It takes bravery to self-express and say what is in your heart. Typically, most people hold onto their feelings or lock them into suppressed resentments and silent grievances. They develop a body armor of tight rigidity to protect them from feeling hurt by others. Yet, doing so can be exhausting, because it takes energy to contain your feelings over time. After a while, it may become impossible to finally say what you are feeling. *Just keep your feelings to yourself in suffering silence.* The result is increased negative energy in the form of resentment, jealousy and blaming. These eventually turn against you and increase your stress and anxiety and susceptibility to disease. One can die in the coffin of one's own body armor.

4. "I wish I kept in touch with my friends."

Humans are social animals and need connection and bonding. Relationships enable us to keep in touch and to tell our stories and past memories to each other. Shared stories often evoke emotional memories and remind us of our rich experiences. Old friends bring up the personal stories that touch us so personally, each time reminding us of our extraordinary lives. By sharing such stories, we also share increased oxytocin and feel more intimately connected and safe. Isolation constricts our life force and leads to physical breakdown and disease.

5. "I wish I allowed myself more pleasure and happiness."

Do you take time every day to give gratitude for your great life and your successes? Do you allow yourself times during the day to indulge your senses and to come alive? Do you create time with close friends and family? Or are you just preoccupied with work and your stresses, upsets and regrets?

It is your choice. Life does not have to run its predictable course of annoyance, blame, resentment and jealousy. Remember, your thoughts give energy and are capable of giving life or taking it.

Regrets and other stresses take their toll on our emotions, health and well-being.

Key Points

- We have been living in a "Death Psychology" for thousands of years

- There is an emerging force of "Immortality Psychology" coming from the radical life extension explorers

- Research from people close to death has opened up some interesting actions people can take that are life giving:
    - a) Be true to yourself
    - b) Reduce your obsession with work
    - c) Express your feelings
    - d) Enhance your friendships
    - e) Seek pleasure and happiness

Chapter 24:

| YOU DESERVE TO LIVE AN EXTRAORDINARY LIFE NOW

Aliveness and well-being require a certain mindset and set of beliefs to sustain a healthy lifestyle. Life Navigators have something to say in this matter. We might want to pay attention to how they shape their beliefs and behaviors to be expressions of vitality, positivity and connection to others. They understand the value of nurturing their Power, Connection and Safety needs and using their brains to better serve their pursuit of living extraordinary lives.

BRAIN TALK

Navigators talk to themselves in a form of "Brain Talk." They have a skill in listening to what their brains are saying and, at the same time, communicate responses to their brains. Our brains want something from us. If we partner with them and satisfy their needs, they respond with tremendous rewards.

Our brains do well with challenge, surprise and discovery. Staying in routine and stuck in a comfort zone does not seem to do much to stimulate the growth of new brain cells. In fact, repetition of old patterns seems to further deepen the neural networks that keep us stuck in redundant patterns of belief and actions; same neural pathways, same results.

Want something else to result? Change your neural networks of thoughts and beliefs. Change and challenge lay down new neural pathways. Through brain plasticity, they provide us with more powerful brains to add value to our lives.

Our brain thrives on exploration and questions. Many Navigators start the day with questions such as, "**What do I want to experience today? What do I want to learn? And what do I want to contribute?**"

These types of open-ended and reflective questions appear to stimulate certain parts of the prefrontal cortex and the release of dopamine.

This morning on my way to work, I reflected on these questions and came up with these answers: "I want to experience peace of mind and ease, learn some options to a business challenge and contribute an open mind to the conversations during the day."

And that was the end to thinking about the day. There was no long thinking or trying to figure out what answers were better or trying to determine the various challenges, problems and concerns that might complicate my day. I simply answered the three questions, briefly reviewed them in my mind and then went through the day living out my answers.

So far, so good! The day is moving along. It is almost 5:00 pm and I am feeling peaceful. I learned some options and still have an open mind. I am loving my day, staying in the present and not getting drawn into whatever negative thoughts might be floating around in my mind or worrying about tomorrow.

LIFE DESIGNERS

Life Navigators are life designers who imagine their futures, create breakthrough strategies and practice actions that increase their personal power, connections to others and sense of safety. They may not think about brain plasticity, epigenesis or the varied appetites of their Computer, Gorilla or Alligator brains, but they grasp the tremendous value of developing power, connection and safety.

For me, today, safety was enhanced by my staying focused on peace of mind and staying at ease no matter what my circumstances turned out to be. I am not sure if I experienced 50 stress points or had 2,000 negative thoughts but, whatever the number, I stayed centered and calm.

Some people around me did not seem to stay calm but that was not my focus for today. In addition, my staying open to options gave me a sense of control and power. I also noticed feeling connected to others by keeping an open mind. I was not attached to any specific outcomes or agendas and was able to understand and validate what others were saying. I think my brain has appreciated my focus for today and has served me well during my discussions, therapy and coaching sessions.

Try the three questions out this week and see if you derive some benefit from asking yourself what you want to experience, learn and contribute.

THE NAVIGATOR'S TOOLKIT

In a previous chapter, I wrote about the Navigator's Toolkit, those specific skills and actions you can take on a daily basis to actually experience Power, Connection and Safety. The following chart outlines some of these tools.

THE NAVIGATOR'S TOOLKIT

POWER	CONNECTION	SAFETY
What is my vision and focus?	Close relationships	Deep breathing (6 breaths per minute)
Why are these important to me?	Relationship with myself	Vivid imagery
3 Questions: Experience, Learn, And Contribute?	Empathy	Meditation
What are my underlying power beliefs?	Listen well	Disarming
What key coping skills do I possess?	Add value to others	5 Gratitudes a day
Learning opportunities today?	Self-talk	Self-care
Write in my victory log	Hugs and touching	Belief management
Keep an open mind and stay curious	Hang with happy people	Run like a sprinter

Use these tools on a daily basis to feed your logical, emotional and survival brains and to keep you present, focused and grounded. When you feel yourself getting pulled off course and into a downward spiral, take a moment to pause and ask yourself what you are experiencing in your thoughts, emotions and body. Then ask yourself if these reactions are serving your vision and purpose. If not, choose one or two of the above tools to help you get back on track. Every time that you pause and shift into a Power, Connection or Safety mode, you increase your brain's resiliency. This makes you the Navigator.

Hopefully, you are curious about living an extraordinary long and healthy life of success, accomplishment and satisfaction and will work every day to enhance your vitality and self-caring. Most of us are masters of the anxious and downward slope of life. But why bother? Try laying down new neural pathways, enhancing your brain functions and lowering anxiety and stress. This translates into a more resilient mind, a healthier body and, hopefully, a longer high-quality life.

While you will sometimes get emotionally hijacked and slip off track, you will get better every day at regaining focus and making your days extraordinary. It is a practice and a great way to play in the game of life. I like to call this way of living the Psychology of Immortality.

As you consider the quality of your life, many of you might not yet have a clear picture of where you are going, how long you want to live or your personal mission that gives life its meaning and purpose. You are not alone or unique. Most people get caught up in the survival part of living, trying to get through the day, rather than creating an immortal life to live into.

But you might consider moving from whatever protective shell or cocoon which houses you and start exploring new opportunities for creating connections and safety with others. Perhaps the power, connection and safety tools described in this book might be a start. Look them over and try some of them out during the day. No one has to know what you're doing, but your body will enjoy the experience.

You no longer have to play the Death Psychology game, a life of reactivity and waiting for something to happen or for someone to rescue you. Get on your surfboard and ride the wave of change that appeals to you. Create a vision that electrifies your body, a purpose to give your life daily meaning.

Rewire your brain and create your immortal identity.

Remember frequently, as I do, that you didn't come here to say goodbye.

Key Points

- Develop your knack for "Brain Talk"

- There is a powerful resource in your brain plasticity

- Your brain thrives on exploration, questions and curiosity

- Be curious

- Be a Life Designer

- Use your Navigator's Toolkit
    - Power Tools
    - Connection Tools
    - Safety Tools

EPILOGUE

ELEPHANTS

How do you make an elephant stay in one spot without wandering away?

Elephants are the largest mammals on the land. Weighing about 10,000 pounds, they stand 13 feet tall, eat several hundred pounds of leaves and branches a day and eliminate almost 60 pounds of waste daily. When push comes to shove, elephants should easily win a strength contest with humans. After all, they can snap a tree in two, crash through a wall and stand up to any animal that tries to challenge them or hurt their offspring.

So why is it that human trainers have succeeded in keeping grown elephants to remain in tight living conditions without heavy bars or iron ankle chains?

One explanation is that trainers lock a tight shackle and chain around the leg of the baby elephant that serves to limit how far it can wander. Step outside the radius of the chain and the baby elephant gets yanked back. After a while he no longer goes any further than the chain permits. He has learned where his comfort zone is and stays inside it even when the chain is later removed. The invisible chain still must feel real to the elephant since he stays fixed in his travel space.

WHAT KEEPS PEOPLE CHAINED AND TRAPPED?

Humans also are chained to stay within a certain distance from their home base. It is not necessarily a physical base, but rather a psychological one where the comfort zone is defined by their thoughts and belief programs.

We are limited by these belief systems unless we realize their boundaries and find ways to shift belief statements into more flexible and far-reaching ones.

Our beliefs keep us stuck.

Our newly created beliefs can set us free.

For example, my college student is stuck in his belief system that he is not good enough. He must be perfect in everything in order to earn respect from others.

Yet, others do not really care one way or the other about his beliefs and his quest for perfection. Unfortunately, even when others enjoy his company and he succeeds in many activities, he feels no satisfaction unless his performance is perfect. Anything less he takes as proof of personal failure.

He spends much time feeling anxious, regretting past "failures" or worrying that life will not turn out well.

He is chained to the belief of not good enough and the quest for perfection. This is his comfort zone and, even though in pain, he finds it difficult to step outside this boundary and just enjoy himself. Recently, we have been focusing on this limiting belief system and experimenting with self-calming strategies. The goal is to allow for risk taking without perfection. He is taking small steps each day, enjoying the experience and giving himself the benefit of doubt. He is practicing keeping note of his actions and considering different ways of looking at what he is doing. He first asks himself how important the result is and what a perfect result would require. He then thinks what the effort would be like if he did it for his own enjoyment. Then he chooses perfection or enjoyment and takes the appropriate action. Applying these strategies, he is reporting much less stress and increased satisfaction. He also is creating a different belief system based on the notion that he is fine and deserves pleasure in his life. No perfection required.

How can an elephant change its belief that it is trapped inside a defined space and move outside its comfort zone?

Perhaps if it accidentally walked outside this zone without feeling the leg pain, that might snap the belief system and allow for more flexible behavior.

Sometimes this works for humans, but stepping outside the belief system can evoke anxiety, which forces the person to quickly retreat.

Our beliefs can be more restrictive and powerful than an elephant's chains.

So what is there to do? Are humans genetically programmed to stay in their fight or flight mode?

Are we trapped inside our Survival or Alligator Brain?

Do we have only the hope of accidental experience to free us from our limited beliefs and ritualistic habits?

Are we stuck in a life of worry, reactivity and waiting for death to finish us off?

BREAKING FREE

There is good news! It is possible to break free of the invisible handcuffs of believing we are not good enough. But this requires a different way of thinking and acting. Breakthrough Thinking and the Navigator's Toolkit provide an approach and resources to change rigid and reactive beliefs and behaviors into more adaptive and creative strategies.

For example, my college student first goes into the Survival Box to calm down his nervous system. He frequently starts by rating his anxiety on a scale of 1-10.

Next, he focuses on his body, scanning himself to locate where his tension is located. Usually, it resides in his chest and stomach. Slow deep breathing into his tense areas activates his parasympathetic nervous system to start its relaxation response.

He is then ready to visualize a more positive situation where he feels safe and cared for. These initial exercises seem to calm him down and allow for clearer problem solving.

He takes another deep breath and a moment to pause and savor the shift in emotion and body sensation. He then looks around in his Toolkit for a Power Tool and answers the four questions for Vision, Purpose, Identity and Actions:

» What do I really desire?

» Why do I want this?

» Who do I have to be to succeed?

» What do I have to do to change my brain?

These questions provide him with a roadmap or GPS to now guide him as he navigates into unfamiliar territory.

GUIDED IMAGERY
Next, he imagines experiencing what he wants with clarity, positive emotion and sees himself behaving the way he desires to be if he could. He would like to be less anxious, more relaxed and just go with the flow of events. This visualization and savoring the experience serve to lay down new neural pathways of a more positive and rewarding nature. Here he lingers in the imagined experience, enjoying behaving in a more relaxed way.

Turning back into his body, he practices posturing, shaping himself into the posture of someone who is comfortable taking actions outside of his comfort zone. This serves to create some body and sensory memory of his desired behavioral change.

He usually chooses the character Indiana Jones with his leather jacket, hat, whip and gun; a little curl of his lip rounds out his impersonation. He is creating his future self, his immortal identity and using it to energize and direct his actions in the moment to live an extraordinary life.

What follows is an answer to two key questions. What new belief could he say to himself to support this new way of perceiving his life? What small action could he now take to support that new belief?

PERFECTIONISM IS SELF-DESTRUCTION

We recently did some belief redesigning around perfection when he complained that he was not doing enough to save the planet. As he spoke, his body tensed up and his speech became somewhat jagged and chaotic. His anxiety level was a nine.

I asked what he would be doing differently if he were saving the planet. He thought he would be contributing full-time without any personal interest to humanity.

I asked him if that implied he should immediately drop out of college, sell all his material goods and move away to a third-world country with no plumbing, electricity or food stores? How about giving up friends, his girlfriend and playing in the college marching band? And he would have to drop out of the community service program he has loved contributing to since he entered college. And, if he were to seek perfect contribution and move to, say, Africa, would he be satisfied if he were then eaten by an alligator?

As we pursued this line of questioning and explored the anticipated losses and potential gains, my client said that this all seemed too extreme. He smiled and realized his perfectionistic thinking about service and sacrifice were causing considerable tension in his body. He recognized these as expressions of perfectionistic thinking and not necessarily living a life of meaningful purpose.

We shifted and again did some deep breathing and imagery work centered on being with friends, playing music and talking to girls. He reported a drop in anxiety and said that he felt connected and loved.

It was clear that the negative consequences of his perfection far outweighed the positive results. But his belief was still strong enough to trigger further guilt. We then used a strategy that Rick Hansen wrote about in *Hardwiring the Brain for Happiness*. He presents the acronym HEAL to represent the following actions:

Have the pleasant experience though imagery and emotion.

Enrich it by lingering for about 20 seconds in the experience. Enjoy the imagined scene.

Absorb it more fully and imagine it flowing throughout your body.

Link the positive experience with the negative one so that the negative belief collapses as the positive one gets stronger. Make sure you keep the positive experience in the foreground. Keep enriching and absorbing it into your consciousness.

My client enjoyed this Power strategy and we have used it during other sessions.

Lately, I have used PSYCH-K, a powerful belief-changing exercise by Rob Williams. It is based on the notion that beliefs are energies that impact the body and its nervous system. Negative beliefs weaken us while positive beliefs strengthen us.

So, the new belief might be, "I am happy and content to just do my best and enjoy the experience." As he repeats this new belief to himself, the exercise is structured to allow full brain absorption and integration.

To learn more about this interesting intervention, check out Rob Williams and PSYCH-K on YouTube.

TEN PIECES OF TRASH
In terms of small actions he could take, he is now picking up ten pieces of trash a day from the ground and throwing them away. He then acknowledges himself for acting in a "green" way and gets on with the day. This action represents a symbolic contribution to the planet and others without moving to a third-world country.

The tools we are using include Power, Safety and Connection exercises that are selected to create a greater sense of safety, competence and being cared about by others. They seem to be turning the tide for him as he reports less anxiety, guilt and obsessive thinking. He is learning how to navigate his inner mind with success, accomplishment and satisfaction. There is nothing to prove and there is no perfection. Life is just a gift to live into, learn and enjoy.

I hope this case example gives you a better idea how to use Breakthrough Thinking and the Power, Connection and Safety Tools to navigate life more effectively. Our Survival Brain is not designed to make life easy for us. It is the best it can be right now as it strives to protect us from danger. It just needs some calming routines to become less agitated and to allow the Computer and Gorilla Brains to help figure out how to live the extraordinary life we all deserve. Fortunately, our brains are highly malleable through neuroplasticity and epigenesis. We have the ability to radically alter our genetic maps and neural associations for our present and future benefit.

We can all enhance the quality of our lives by learning to become Navigators. While we might get pulled into Survivor and Victim thinking and triggered by situations or thoughts, we are not chained into a reactive lifestyle.

We can become more aware, breathe into our bodies, and use our creative minds to enjoy the extraordinary life we all deserve. In this vision, we may live healthier and more productive lives and be around in the near future to benefit from the medical and technological advances to counteract the aging and disease process.

Remember, we did not come to say goodbye!

ADDENDUM

BREAKTHROUGH EXERCISES FOR LIVING AN EXTRAORDINARY LIFE

Here are four extraordinary exercises to try out as a way to experience from an imaginative or right-brain perspective some of the key ideas in this book.

The first is a GRATITUDE EXERCISE that you might appreciate as a 125-year-old person who is practicing Breakthrough Thinking.

The second, FEEDING YOUR HUNGRY BRAINS, is designed to give you an experience of integrated brain problem solving.

The third is called The NEGOTIATION EXERCISE, which is about managing competing desires between your brains, while the fourth is an emotionally touching exercise called MEETING YOUR IMMORTAL SELF. Good luck!

1. Your Gratitude and Acknowledgment Celebration for Living an Extraordinary Life at Age 125 years

Find a quiet time and move into a relaxation mode. Take several deep breaths, let go of tension as you breathe in relaxation and peace. Imagine a time or situation in which you felt calm, safe and cared for. Step into that experience and begin to relive it. Let yourself go and breathe into it.

As you let yourself go and move into peace and safety, imagine that you are now age 125, feeling strong and vital. You have taken care of yourself and crafted your beliefs into living a life of a Navigator: clear vision, goals that reflect your vision, taking daily actions to live your dream and be resilient. No matter what, you are following your True North.

Imagine a celebration that your loved ones and friends have coordinated to acknowledge you as a Life Navigator. A person who has taken care of himself, developed beliefs derived from love and growth, and fed his three brains the emotional foods they crave: Power, Connection and Safety. You are now 125 years old, but feel and look 40. Your friends, family and colleagues are meeting to celebrate you as a Navigator, someone living a Breakthrough Life of success, accomplishment and great satisfaction. You have been an early adapter of creating a life in which you are thriving and are an inspiration to others.

You are standing in front of about 250 people who love and respect you. You wish to express your gratitude and appreciation for having launched yourself into a life of

Navigation and being an early adapter of radical life extension. It is clear to you that you will live longer and younger every year, regardless of what others think. You have created a belief system based on positive psychology, continued passion and extraordinary living. Your body and health are an expression of vitality, growth and resilience. You also have taken advantage of medical breakthroughs that have eliminated or reversed illnesses associated with the aging process. Every day you are getting stronger.

Imagine that you are now talking to your kinship or cohort group about what you have experienced, grappled with and learned so far about living an extraordinary life.

What do you want to share with them from a place of sincere and heartfelt gratitude, respect and generosity? Your Wolf of Love is fully present and you are making a contribution to all who you love and value. Originate from a place of generosity and compassion.

What are the three most important things you want to share with them? As you share, picture their loving expressions. Feel the love and admiration in your body. Its warmth touches your heart and lifts your spirits. Express your love and gratitude to your special people and see the tears of joy come to their eyes.

2. Feeding Your Hungry Brains Exercise

Most people, more than 95 percent, probably have very little or no idea what we are talking about here.

You now know the value of understanding your three different brains that have developed over the last 400 million years. With the knowledge of neuroplasticity combined with the power of belief, freely explore your next strategy to create internal peace and calm.

With you and your three brains highly connected, you are faced with an interesting challenge.

All throughout time, your three brains — Computer, Gorilla and Alligator — have been competing for your attention, much like three siblings vying for their parental attention. Although your Wolf of Anger is urging you to put these three brains in their place and to apply sternness, you choose instead to feed your Wolf of Love. Your Wolf of Love is secure, confident, caring and compassionate.

Imagine you now are sitting down in a room with your competing Computer, Gorilla and Alligator and are clear that you want to help them to work together. In this endeavor, they all either thrive or perish.

» What do you want them to know about your commitment to each of them?

» How do you value and appreciate how each has contributed to your great life?

» What is it you want them to know about the joint work that lies ahead so that all can thrive, achieve, feel safe and be successful?

Alone, they each are incomplete. They need someone to pull them together toward a shared vision. What is it you want to tell them that could inspire increased trust, love and partnership that might help these three brains to better integrate together and support your vision to live an extraordinary life?

Ask each what it needs from you to feel seen, acknowledged and valued.

Thank each for its unique contribution to your life and affirm you are conscious of giving them what they need to partner with you in your life journey.

Be and act like a Navigator.

3. The Negotiation

Imagine Your Alligator and Gorilla brains are not getting along. Alligator wants you to not get involved in a new relationship. It is fearful that you will get hurt and end up depressed and scared again, just like what you went through as a teenager many years ago. It wants you to run away and kill off your emerging love connection.

Meanwhile, your Gorilla Brain is hungry for love and connection. It is urging you to get involved and bond. To love and have lost is more important than never to have loved at all, it reminds you.

As this battle to love or run is ensuing, your Computer Brain is watching and trying to figure out what you should do: love or leave.

Both the Alligator and Gorilla in you are trying to convince your Computer to agree with its point of view. What does your Computer have to say? It is the most thoughtful, but the youngest of your three brains. Now is the time to speak up. What does it have to say that might help to resolve this internal argument?

Maybe it does not know how to help. So, you take the lead and acknowledge that the Computer is trying to help but can't quite get the job done.

Acknowledge the longing your Gorilla Brain feels in its quest for love.

Be compassionate with your scared Alligator Brain for its fear of being hurt.

Think with them about how they can help each other to succeed and what you could do to help all three to work together.

» What did you notice during these visualization exercises? Any surprises?

» Could you experience the different voices in each brain?

» Any luck in negotiating conflict between your emotional and survival brains?

» Was the conflict too much for the problem-solving brain to handle?

4. Meeting Your Immortal Self

This can be the most extraordinary exercise you can do. I introduced this exercise at People Unlimited, a social and educational organization focused on radical life extension based in Scottsdale, AZ. There were about 150 people who experienced this experimental exercise and many were deeply touched and changed by their experiences. One participant was so moved she composed a poem which she later recited to the whole group.

Here is the exercise:

Find a quiet time and sit in a comfortable chair. Turn off your cell phone and computer. This is your time and no one is allowed to interrupt.

Take several slow, deep breaths and let yourself let go of any concerns or things you think you have to do.

Feel your body being held by the chair.

Pay attention to your body, first the facial muscles around your mouth and jaw. Notice any tension in your neck, then your chest and stomach.

Feel yourself breathing as your abdomen rises and falls with each breath.

Continue to relax and let go.

Now imagine a soft, white cloud the shape of a chair is caressing your body and carrying you to a place where you love to be, perhaps the beach, a forest or a valley glen.

As you arrive, look around and take in the beauty, the sounds and the aromas. Breathe it all in and feel the pleasure as your body responds with increased relaxation.

You hear a voice calling your name. Walk toward it. You have heard this soft, inviting voice before; it sounds comfortable and familiar. As you walk toward it, you notice how quiet and lovely everything appears.

In the distance, you see a figure beckoning you on. You continue walking closer. As you do, you see his or her warm smile drawing you forward.

You walk and stand in front of this figure and you take in a glowing sense of connection and safety. You smile back as the figure says, "I've been waiting a long time to see you. I've missed you. I am glad you are here."

The figure looks like you, except stronger, more vital. You feel his or her love and caring. You experience love and caring back.

You take another deep breath and let go of any remaining tension. As you gaze into your figure's eyes, you realize it is you in the future, your Immortal Self.

Your Immortal Self acknowledges your experiences as you moved from being a Victim or Survivor into the world of a Life Navigator. The figure expresses gratitude and appreciation for your courage and willingness to live into your vision and dream. It acknowledges your emotional pain, the challenges you faced and the people to which you felt most connected. It expresses joy and pride in who you are and thanks you for allowing it to thrive in your life.

You touch each other's face, smile and warmly embrace. As you do, you feel yourself letting go, merging into your Immortal Self. You feel the energy and vitality of your immortal being throughout your body and rejoice in the experience.

Let yourself experience the fullness of the moment: the love, connection, the physical vitality and the awareness that you are immortal and perfect just the way you are. Breathe it all in.

When you are ready, thank and give gratitude to your Immortal Being, then embrace and say goodbye.

Take another deep breath and return to the place where you are sitting.

You now are carrying your Immortal Self with you and feel it stirring in your heart and body.

You are revitalized and fully alive.

You are an Immortal Being.

In summary, these four exercises are designed to lift you out of your usual and predictable way of thinking and experiencing your life. They are breakthrough exercises which can transport you into the Breakthrough Zone of redesigning your psychology and giving you a sense of your own immortality.

While we are not yet in the zone of actual physical immortality where there is no longer personal death, that time is coming.

As Bob Dylan put it, "The times they are a-changing."

The key here is to experience your psychological immortality, to create beliefs and actions that revitalize your life, enabling you to move into a radically long life beyond your predicted death.

As you transcend the standard belief of gradual decline and eventual death, a new life will begin to open up. If you create it first, it will manifest soon afterwards.

Change your brain, change your life.

Change your life and become a Life Navigator.

Vision | By Lorna Collett

Luminescent body of light...
Effervescent fire of life...
Lean-limbed, golden-skinned beauty...
Secure, fearless, free.
Aura of joy palpable, visceral...
My future self smiles at me.

Her expression of gratitude penetrates my defenses...
The old familiar self buckles under the depth
of compassion that is this being's core.
I drink in her appreciation and praise as fresh nectar...
I am fortified by the conviction that propelled us
to the future.

Face to face with the Creator...
I surrender to the magical vision before me.
Time and distance melting away in the fusion
of our embrace...
As two become one.

I revel in the now, at rest in the vastness of all
that is to come…
Future and present woven together,
A tapestry of endless possibilities…
Eternity in the making.

Comes time to plant ourselves forever…
And blossom to the glory of all we are to be…
Hold not our visions as gods before us,
*For our future selves are blessed by **our** boldness **this day**…*
Go forth clear in the choices of creation…
We are the future now.

REFERENCES

Anderson et al. (2012). *Health Span Approximates Lifespan Among Supercentenarians.* J Gerontol, A 67 A

J. Bowlby (1973). *Attachment and Loss.* Basic Books

W. Bridges (1991). *Managing Transitions.* Addison Wesley

CNN (2001)

CDC (2013). *Birth Trends.* A Roberts. (2015) CNN

S. Cole (Dobbs, 2013). *The Social Life of Genes,* Pacific Standard

A. Crouch (2010). *10 Most Significant Cultural Trends of the Last Decade*

J. Dispenza (2012)

M. Emoto (2008). *Messages From Water.*

S. Goodman (2011)

S. Goodman (2016). *The Centenarian.*

R. Hanson, *Hardwiring Happiness.*

H. Harlow (1961). *The Development of Affectional Patterns in Infant Monkeys.* B.M. Foss (ed.), Determinants of Infant Behavior Vol. 1, London, Wiley

J. Kehoe (2010)

D. Kekich (2012). *Smart, Strong and Sexy at 100?*

E. Langer (2009)

R. Lang, Urban Sociologist and University of Nevada.

B. Lipton (1990). *The Biology of Belief*

Jim Loehr and Tony Schwan (2003). *The Power of Full Engagement.* Simon and Shuster

P. Lynch and P. Kordis (1989). *Strategy of the Dolphin.* A Selfware Book

National Statistics Report Vol. 50, No. 6, *Life Expectancy at Birth by Race and Sex*

R. Sapolsky (2004). *Why Zebras Don't Get Ulcers.*

J. Read Hawthorne (2014). *Words To Live* By, Blog Post

S. Reinberg (2011). *Judo of the Soul: The Art of Psychic Self-Defense.* Healthy News

D. Siegel (2009). *Mindsight: The New Science of Personal Transformation*

R. Spitz (1950). *Anxiety In Infancy.* Int. J. Psycho- Analysis 311

B. Ware (2012). *The Top Five Regrets of the Dying*

R. Williams, *The Psychology of Change*

ABOUT THE AUTHOR

Moss Jackson, Ph.D. is a clinical psychologist in private practice in Ardmore, Pennsylvania. He works with teenagers, adults and couples, and coaches people to live successful lives as Life Navigators.

Moss has written four self-published books and is not yet a best-selling author but is confident that his vision will soon be realized.

He and another writer, Joe Bardin, have co-authored a film script, *If My Mother Is Dead, Why Am I Still Arguing With Her?* They are now looking for someone in the film industry to take on this project.

Moss' other books are:

Navigating for Success: Passion, Goals and Action, 2010

52 Things You Need to Know About Partnerships, 2011

Making a Success of Our Family Business Succession Planning, co-authored with David Franzetta, 2012

Recruiting: The Art of the Interview, 2011

How to Contact Dr. Jackson

For book orders, coaching, to attend one of his workshops, or just to connect:

ADDRESS:	125 Coulter Avenue, Ardmore, PA 19003
EMAIL:	mossalan@aol.com
WEB:	www.navigatingforsuccess.com
PHONE:	610-642-4873 ext. 23

We live in an exciting time as we push the boundaries of our known world. Biotechnology, nanotechnology, artificial intelligence, 3-D organ printing and stem cell research may take us into lives of 200, 500 or even 1,000 years. This is a voyage of breakthroughs into a new world that will require powerful thinking, careful research and ethical considerations.

Only time will tell where we end up.

MOSS JACKSON, Ph.D.

• —— | • | • | • | —— •